"An amazing piece of theater. . . . Out of the Shepard tragedy is wrenched art." —*The New York Post*

"A complex and ultimately optimistic portrait of a town that was challenged by the most catastrophic of events." —*USA Today*

"Sad, sober and gripping. . . . Something nourishing has been excavated by Kaufman and his committed collaborators from the tragedy." —*Daily Variety*

"A towering theatrical accomplishment. . . . [*The Laramie Project* is] *Our Town* for the new millennium, capturing from real life the same sense of humanity in the raw that Thornton Wilder did years ago with the fictional Grover's Corner. The play moves the theater in a new and different direction." —*San Francisco Times*

"An invigorating theatrical adventure." —David Rothenberg

Praise for

THE LARAMIE PROJECT: TEN YEARS LATER

"Rekindles all the anger and heartbreak. . . . Illuminates with disturbing clarity how sharply attitudes toward the killing have changed in Laramie, how a revised history has gradually replaced the facts of the case, once undisputed." —*The New York Times*

"Moving. . . . One feels one's sympathies shifting and deepening as the voices of those we met in the original piece—and some new ones—ruminate upon the meaning of Shepard's death."
—*Chicago Tribune*

"A powerful script." —*The Austin Chronicle*

THE
LARAMIE PROJECT

AND

THE
LARAMIE PROJECT:
TEN YEARS LATER

ALSO BY MOISÉS KAUFMAN

Gross Indecency: The Three Trials of Oscar Wilde

33 Variations

THE
LARAMIE PROJECT

Moisés Kaufman
and Members of
Tectonic Theater Project

AND

THE
LARAMIE PROJECT:
TEN YEARS LATER

Moisés Kaufman,
Leigh Fondakowski,
Greg Pierotti, Andy Paris,
and Stephen Belber

VINTAGE BOOKS

A DIVISION OF RANDOM HOUSE LLC

NEW YORK

VINTAGE BOOKS EDITIONS, 2001, 2014

Copyright © 2001, 2014 by Moisés Kaufman

All rights reserved. Published in the United States by Vintage Books, a division
of Random House LLC, New York, a Penguin Random House company.
Originally published in slightly different form by Vintage Books, a division of
Random House LLC, New York, in 2004.

Vintage and colophon are trademarks of Random House LLC.

The U.S. West World Premiere was produced by The Denver Center Theatre Company,
Donovan Marley, Artistic Director, in association with Tectonic Theater Project, Moisés
Kaufman, Artistic Director.

Originally produced in New York City at the Union Square Theatre by Roy Gabay
and Tectonic Theater Project in association with Gayle Francis and the Araca Group.
Associate Producers: Mara Isaacs and Hart Sharp Entertainment.

The Laramie Project was developed in part with the support of the
Sundance Theatre Laboratory.

The Cataloging-in-Publication Data is on file at the Library of Congress.

Vintage Trade Paperback ISBN: 978-0-8041-7039-0
eBook ISBN: 978-0-8041-7040-6

www.vintagebooks.com

Printed in the United States of America
10 9 8 7 6 5

*Dedicated to the people of Laramie, Wyoming,
and to Matthew Shepard*

THE
LARAMIE PROJECT

Moisés Kaufman
and Members of
Tectonic Theater Project

Head Writer	Leigh Fondakowski
Associate Writers	Stephen Belber, Greg Pierotti,
	Stephen Wangh
Dramaturgs	Amanda Gronich,
	Sarah Lambert, John McAdams,
	Maude Mitchell, Andy Paris,
	Barbara Pitts, Kelli Simpkins

INTRODUCTION
by Moisés Kaufman

After all, not to create only, or found only,
But to bring perhaps from afar what is already founded,
To give it our own identity, average, limitless, free.

WALT WHITMAN

There are moments in history when a particular event brings the various ideologies and beliefs prevailing in a culture into sharp focus. At these junctures the event becomes a lightning rod of sorts, attracting and distilling the essence of these philosophies and convictions. By paying careful attention in moments like this to people's words, one is able to hear the way these prevailing ideas affect not only individual lives but also the culture at large.

The trials of Oscar Wilde were such an event. When I read the transcripts of the trials (while preparing to write *Gross Indecency*), I was struck by the clarity with which they illuminated an entire culture. In these pages one can see not only a community dealing with the problem that Wilde presented but, in their own words, Victorian men and women telling us—three generations later—

about the ideologies, idiosyncrasies, and philosophies that formed the pillars of that culture and ruled their lives.

The brutal murder of Matthew Shepard was another event of this kind. In its immediate aftermath, the nation launched into a dialogue that brought to the surface how we think and talk about homosexuality, sexual politics, education, class, violence, privileges and rights, and the difference between tolerance and acceptance.

The idea of *The Laramie Project* originated in my desire to learn more about why Matthew Shepard was murdered, about what happened that night, about the town of Laramie. The idea of listening to the citizens talk really interested me. How is Laramie different from the rest of the country, and how is it similar?

Shortly after the murder, I posed the question to my company, Tectonic Theater Project. What can we as theater artists do as a response to this incident? And, more concretely, is theater a medium that can contribute to the national dialogue on current events?

These concerns fall squarely within Tectonic Theater Project's mission. Every project we undertake as a company has two objectives: (1) to examine the subject matter at hand, and (2) to explore theatrical language and form. In an age when film and television are constantly redefining and refining their tools and devices, the theater has too often remained entrenched in the nineteenth-century traditions of realism and naturalism. In this sense, our interest was to continue to have a dialogue on both how the theater speaks and how it is created. Thus, I was very interested in this model: A theater company travels somewhere, talks to people, and returns with what it saw and heard to create a play.

At the time I also happened to run across a Brecht essay I had not read in a long time, "The Street Scene." In it Brecht uses as a model the following situation: "an eyewitness demonstrating to a collection of people how a traffic accident took place." He goes on to build a theory about his "epic theatre" based on this model. The essay gave me an idea about how to deal with this project, in terms of both its creation and its aesthetic vocabulary.

So in November 1998, four weeks after the murder of Matthew Shepard, nine members of Tectonic Theater Project and I traveled to Laramie, Wyoming, to collect interviews that might become material for a play. Little did we know that we would devote two years of our lives to this project. We returned to Laramie many times over the course of the next year and a half and conducted more than two hundred interviews.

This play opened in Denver at the Denver Center Theater. Then it moved to New York City, to the Union Square Theatre. And in November 2000 we took the play to Laramie.

The experience of working on *The Laramie Project* has been one of great sadness, great beauty, and, perhaps most important, great revelations—about our nation, about our ideas, about ourselves.

A NOTE FROM MOISÉS KAUFMAN

The Laramie Project was written through a unique collaboration by Tectonic Theater Project. During the year-and-a-half-long development of the play, members of the company and I traveled to Laramie six times to conduct interviews with the people of the town. We transcribed and edited the interviews, then conducted several workshops in which the members of the company presented material and acted as dramaturgs in the creation of the play.

As the volume of material grew with each trip to Laramie, a small writers' group from within the company began to work closely with me to further organize and edit the material, conduct additional research in Laramie, and collaborate on the writing of the play. This group was led by Leigh Fondakowski as head writer, with Stephen Belber and Greg Pierotti as associate writers.

As we got closer to the play's first production in Denver, the actors, including Stephen Belber and Greg Pierotti, turned their focus to performance while Leigh Fondakowski continued to work with me on drafts of the play, as did Stephen Wangh, who by then had joined us as an associate writer and "bench coach."

The Laramie Project received its world premiere at The Ricketson Theatre by the Denver Center Theatre Company (Donovan Marley, Artistic Director) in association with Tectonic Theater Project (Moisés Kaufman, Artistic Director; Jeffrey LaHoste, Managing Director) in Denver, Colorado, on February 19, 2000. It was directed by Moisés Kaufman; the set design was by Robert Brill; the lighting design was by Betsy Adams; the original music was by Peter Golub; the sound design was by Craig Breitenbach; the video and slides were by Martha Swetzoff; the costume design was by Moe Schell; the assistant director was Leigh Fondakowski; and the Project Advisor was Stephen Wangh. The cast was as follows:

Stephen Belber: Himself, Doc O'Connor, Matt Galloway, Anonymous Friend of Aaron McKinney, Bill McKinney, Andrew Gomez, Fred Phelps, Mormon Spiritual Advisor, Conrad Miller, Narrator, Ensemble.

Amanda Gronich: Herself, Eileen Engen (Act One), Marge Murray, Baptist Minister, Trish Steger, Shadow, Newsperson, Narrator, Ensemble.

Mercedes Herrero: Reggie Fluty, Rebecca Hilliker, Waitress, Newsperson, Narrator, Ensemble.

John McAdams: Moisés Kaufman, Philip Dubois (Act One), Stephen Mead Johnson, Murdock Cooper, Jon Peacock, Dennis Shepard, Harry Woods, Narrator, Ensemble.

Andy Paris: Himself, Jedadiah Schultz, Doug Laws, Dr. Cantway, Matt Mickelson, Russell Henderson, Aaron McKinney, Philip Dubois (Act Two), Kerry Drake, Narrator, Ensemble.

Greg Pierotti: Himself, Sgt. Hing, Phil LaBrie, Father Roger Schmit, Rulon Stacey, Detective Sgt. Rob DeBree, Jonas Slonaker, Narrator, Ensemble.

Barbara Pitts: Herself, Catherine Connolly, April Silva, Zubaida Ula, Sherry Aanenson, Lucy Thompson, Eileen Engen (Act Two), Narrator, Ensemble.

Kelli Simpkins: Leigh Fondakowski, Zackie Salmon, Alison Sears, Romaine Patterson, Aaron Kreifels, Tiffany Edwards, Narrator, Ensemble.

The Laramie Project subsequently opened Off-Broadway at The Union Square Theatre (Alan J. Schuster and Margaret Cotter, Managing Directors) in New York City on May 18, 2000. It was produced by Roy Gabay and Tectonic Theater Project in association with Gayle Francis and the Araca Group; Associate Producers Mara Isaacs and Hart Sharp Entertainment. It was directed by Moisés Kaufman; the set design was by Robert Brill; the lighting design was by Betsy Adams; the original music was by Peter Golub; the video and slides were by Martha Swetzoff; the costume design was by Moe Schell; the assistant director was Leigh Fondakowski; and the Project Advisor was Stephen Wangh. The cast was as follows:

Stephen Belber: Himself, Doc O'Connor, Matt Galloway, Anonymous Friend of Aaron McKinney, Bill McKinney, Andrew Gomez, Fred Phelps, Mormon Spiritual Advisor, Conrad Miller, Narrator, Ensemble.

Amanda Gronich: Herself, Eileen Engen (Act One), Marge Murray, Baptist Minister, Trish Steger, Shadow, Newsperson, Narrator, Ensemble.

Mercedes Herrero: Reggie Fluty, Rebecca Hilliker, Waitress, Newsperson, Narrator, Ensemble.

John McAdams: Moisés Kaufman, Philip Dubois (Act One), Stephen Mead Johnson, Murdock Cooper, Jon Peacock, Dennis Shepard, Harry Woods, Narrator, Ensemble.

Andy Paris: Himself, Jedadiah Schultz, Doug Laws, Dr. Cantway, Matt Mickelson, Russell Henderson, Aaron McKinney, Philip Dubois (Act Two), Kerry Drake, Narrator, Ensemble.

Greg Pierotti: Himself, Sgt. Hing, Phil LaBrie, Father Roger Schmit, Rulon Stacey, Detective Sgt. Rob DeBree, Jonas Slonaker, Narrator, Ensemble.

Barbara Pitts: Herself, Catherine Connolly, April Silva, Zubaida Ula, Sherry Aanenson, Lucy Thompson, Eileen Engen (Act Two), Narrator, Ensemble.

Kelli Simpkins: Leigh Fondakowski, Zackie Salmon, Alison Sears, Romaine Patterson, Aaron Kreifels, Tiffany Edwards, Narrator, Ensemble.

THE LARAMIE PROJECT CHARACTERS

Aaron Kreifels—University student; nineteen years old.

Aaron McKinney—One of the perpetrators; a roofer; twenty-one years old.

Alison Mears—Volunteer for a social service agency in town; very good friend of Marge Murray; fifties.

Amanda Gronich—Member of Tectonic Theater Project.

Andrew Gomez—Latino homeboy from Laramie; twenties.

Andy Paris—Member of Tectonic Theater Project.

Anonymous—Friend of Aaron McKinney's; formerly into drugs but has turned his life around; works for the railroad; twenties.

April Silva—Bisexual university student; nineteen years old.

Bailiff

Baptist Minister—Originally from Texas; fifties.

Baptist Minister's wife—late forties.

Barbara Pitts—Member of Tectonic Theater Project.

Bill McKinney—Father of Aaron McKinney; truck driver; forties.

Cal Rerucha—Prosecuting attorney; has a slight stutter; fifties.

Catherine Connolly—Out lesbian professor at the university; analytical; forties.

Conrad Miller—Car mechanic; thirties.

Dennis Shepard—Father of Matthew Shepard; Wyoming native; forties.

Doc O'Connor—Limousine driver and local entrepreneur; fifties.

Doug Laws—State Ecclesiastical leader for the Mormon Church in Laramie; a professor at the University of Wyoming; fifties.

Dr. Cantway—Emergency room doctor at Ivinson Memorial Hospital in Laramie; fifties.

E-mail Sender

Father Roger Schmit—Catholic priest; very outspoken; wide vocal range and varied timbre; forties.

Gene Pratt—Russell Henderson's Mormon home teacher.

Gil and Eileen Engen—Ranchers; he is in his sixties; she is in her fifties.

Governor Jim Geringer—Republican governor; a public figure; wears a cowboy hat; forty-five years old.

Greg Pierotti—Member of Tectonic Theater Project.

Harry Woods—Gay university employee; fifty-two years old.

Jedadiah Schultz—University student; nineteen years old.

Jeffrey Lockwood—Laramie resident, very involved in local politics; forties.

Jen—A friend of Aaron McKinney; twenties.

Jon Peacock—Matthew's academic advisor; political science professor; late thirties.

Jonas Slonaker—Gay man; moved to Laramie from a larger city; flannel shirts and jeans; forties.

Jurors and Foreperson

Kerry Drake—Reporter with the Caspar *Star Tribune*; forties.

Kristin Price—Girlfriend of Aaron McKinney; has a son with Aaron; Tennessee accent; young, in her twenties.

Leigh Fondakowski—Member of Tectonic Theater Project.

Lucy Thompson—Grandmother of Russell Henderson; working-class woman who provided a popular day-care service for the town; sixties.

Marge Murray—Reggie's mother; she has had emphysema from many years of smoking but continues to smoke; seventies.

Matt Galloway—Bartender at the Fireside Bar; student at
the University of Wyoming; bartending the night that
Matthew Shepard was kidnapped from the Fireside;
twenties.

Matt Mickelson—Owner of the Fireside; worn-out cowboy hat
that rides low on his head; thirties.

Media/newspaper people

Moisés Kaufman—Member of Tectonic Theater Project.

Murdock Cooper—Rancher; resident of Centennial, a nearby
town; fifties.

Officer Reggie Fluty—The policewoman who responded to
the 911 call and discovered Matthew at the fence;
forties.

Phil Labrie—A friend of Matthew Shepard; Eastern European
accent; late twenties.

Phillip Dubois—President of the University of Wyoming; priest
at the funeral; forties.

Priest—Priest at Mattew shepard's funeral.

Rebecca Hilliker—Head of the theater department at the
University of Wyoming; Midwest accent; forties.

Reverend Fred Phelps—Minister from Kansas; his website is
Godhatesfags.com; sixties.

Rob DeBree—Detective Sergeant for the Albany County
Sheriff's department; chief investigator for the Matthew
Shepard murder; very deep voice; has become a national
advocate for hate crime legislation as a result of his
involvement with the case; forties.

Romaine Patterson—Very young lesbian; energetic; leather
jacket; twenty-one years old.

Rulon Stacey—CEO Poudre Valley Hospital in Fort Collins,
Colorado; Mormon; a gentle and compassionate family
man; forties.

Russell Henderson—One of the perpetrators; twenties.

Sergeant Hing—Detective at the Laramie Police Department; forties.

Shadow—DJ at the Fireside; African American man; thirty years old.

Shannon—A friend of Aaron McKinney; male; twenties.

Sherry Aanenson—Russell Henderson's landlord; educated at the University of Wyoming, but because of Laramie's poor economy she was working as a waitress when we met her; forties.

Sherry Johnson—Administrative assistant at the university; forties.

Stephen Belber—Member of Tectonic Theater Project.

Stephen Mead Johnson—Unitarian minister; wry, ironical; fifties.

Tiffany Edwards—Local reporter; just out of college when this hit; full of energy; twenties.

Trish Steger—Romaine's sister; owner of a shop in town; very active in local politics; opinionated; forties.

Two Judges

Waitress—Looks like Debbie Reynolds.

Zackie Salmon—Administrator at the University of Wyoming; originally from Texas; thick accent; her emotions are very raw and always close to the surface; forties.

Zubaida Ula—Muslim woman in Laramie; an inquisitive mind; passionate; twenties.

NOTE: When a character's name is not given (e.g., "Friend of Aaron McKinney's," "Baptist Minister," etc.), it is at the person's request.

ABOUT THE STAGING

The set is a performance space. There are a few tables and chairs. Costumes and props are always visible. The basic costumes are the ones worn by the company of actors. Costumes to portray the people of Laramie should be simple: a shirt, a pair of glasses, a hat. The desire is to suggest, not re-create. Along the same lines, this should be an actor-driven event. Costume changes, set changes, and anything else that happens on the stage should be done by the company of actors.

ABOUT THE TEXT

When writing this play, we used a technique that Moisés originated called "moment work." It is a method to create and analyze theater from a structuralist (or "tectonic") perspective. For that reason, there are no "scenes" in this play, only "moments." A "moment" does not mean a change of locale or an entrance or exit of actors or characters. It is simply a unit of theatrical time, a unit which is then juxtaposed with other units to convey meaning.

PLACE:

Laramie, Wyoming, U.S.A.

TIME:

1998–1999

ACT I

MOMENT: A DEFINITION

NARRATOR: On November fourteenth, nineteen ninety-eight, the members of Tectonic Theater Project traveled to Laramie, Wyoming, and conducted interviews with the people of the town. During the next year, we would return to Laramie several times and conduct over two hundred interviews. The play you are about to see is edited from those interviews, as well as from journal entries by members of the company and other found texts. Company member Greg Pierotti.

GREG PIEROTTI: My first interview was with Detective Sergeant Hing of the Laramie Police Department. At the start of the interview he was sitting behind his desk, sitting something like this *(he transforms into Sergeant Hing)*:

I was born and raised here.
    My family is, uh, third generation.
    My grandparents moved here in the early nineteen hundreds.
    We've had basically three, well, my daughter makes it fourth generation.

Quite a while. . . . It's a good place to live. Good people—
lots of space.

Now, all the towns in southern Wyoming are laid out and
spaced because of the railroad came through. It was how far
they could go before having to refuel and rewater. And, uh,
Laramie was a major stopping point. That's why the towns
are spaced so far apart. We're one of the largest states in the
country, and the least populated.

REBECCA HILLIKER: There's so much space between people and
towns here, so much time for reflection.

NARRATOR: Rebecca Hilliker, head of the theater department at
the University of Wyoming.

REBECCA HILLIKER: You have an opportunity to be happy in your
life here. I found that people here were nicer than in the Midwest, where I used to teach, because they were happy. They
were glad the sun was shining. And it shines a lot here.

SERGEANT HING: What you have is, you have your old-time
traditional-type ranchers, they've been here forever—Laramie's
been the hub of where they come for their supplies and stuff
like that.

EILEEN ENGEN: Stewardship is one thing all our ancestors taught
us.

NARRATOR: Eileen Engen, rancher.

EILEEN ENGEN: If you don't take care of the land, then you ruin it
and you lose your living. So you first of all have to take care
of your land and do everything you can to improve it.

DOC O'CONNOR: I love it here.

NARRATOR: Doc O'Connor, limousine driver.

DOC O'CONNOR: You couldn't put me back in that mess out there back east. Best thing about it is the climate. The cold, the wind. They say the Wyoming wind'll drive a man insane. But you know what? It don't bother me. Well, some of the times it bothers me. But most of the time it don't.

SERGEANT HING: And then you got uh, the university population.

PHILIP DUBOIS: I moved here after living in a couple of big cities.

NARRATOR: Philip Dubois, president of the University of Wyoming.

PHILIP DUBOIS: I loved it there. But you'd have to be out of your mind to let your kids out after dark. And here, in the summertime, my kids play out at night till eleven and I don't think twice about it.

SERGEANT HING: And then you have the people who live in Laramie, basically.

ZACKIE SALMON: I moved here from rural Texas.

NARRATOR: Zackie Salmon, Laramie resident.

ZACKIE SALMON: Now, in Laramie, if you don't know a person, you will definitely know someone they know. So it can only be one degree removed at most. And for me—I love it! I mean, I love to go to the grocery store 'cause I get to visit with four or five or six people every time I go. And I don't really mind people knowing my business—'cause what's my business? I mean, my business is basically good.

DOC O'CONNOR: I like the trains, too. They don't bother me. Well, some of the times they bother me, but most times they don't. Even though one goes by every thirteen minutes out where I live. . . .

NARRATOR: Doc actually lives up in Bossler. But everybody in Laramie knows him. He's also not really a doctor.

DOC O'CONNOR: They used to carry cattle . . . them trains. Now all they carry is diapers and cars.

APRIL SILVA: I grew up in Cody, Wyoming.

NARRATOR: April Silva, university student.

APRIL SILVA: Laramie is better than where I grew up. I'll give it that.

SERGEANT HING: It's a good place to live. Good people, lots of space. Now, when the incident happened with that boy, a lot of press people came here. And one time some of them followed me out to the crime scene. And uh, well, it was a beautiful day, absolutely gorgeous day, real clear and crisp and the sky was that blue that, uh . . . you know, you'll never be able to paint, it's just sky blue—it's just gorgeous. And the mountains in the background and a little snow on 'em, and this one reporter, uh, lady . . . person, that was out there, she said . . .

REPORTER: Well, who found the boy, who was out here anyway?

SERGEANT HING: And I said, "Well, this is a really popular area for people to run, and mountain biking's really big out here, horseback riding, it's just, well, it's close to town." And she looked at me and she said:

REPORTER: Who in the hell would want to run out here?

SERGEANT HING: And I'm thinking, "Lady, you're just missing the point." You know, all you got to do is turn around, see the mountains, smell the air, just take in what's around you. And they were just—nothing but the story. I didn't feel judged, I felt that they were stupid. They're, they're missing the point—they're just missing the whole point.

JEDADIAH SCHULTZ: It's hard to talk about Laramie now, to tell you what Laramie is, for us.

NARRATOR: Jedadiah Schultz, university student.

JEDADIAH SCHULTZ: If you would have asked me before, I would have told you Laramie is a beautiful town, secluded enough that you can have your own identity. . . . A town with a strong sense of community—everyone knows everyone. . . . A town with a personality that most larger cities are stripped of. Now, after Matthew, I would say that Laramie is a town defined by an accident, a crime. We've become Waco, we've become Jasper. We're a noun, a definition, a sign!

MOMENT: JOURNAL ENTRIES

NARRATOR: Journal entries—members of the company. Andy Paris.

ANDY PARIS: Moisés called saying he had an idea for his next theater project. But there was a somberness to his voice, so I asked what it was all about and he told me he wanted to do a piece about what's happening in Wyoming.

NARRATOR: Stephen Belber.

STEPHEN BELBER: Leigh told me the company was thinking of going out to Laramie to conduct interviews and that they wanted me to come. But I'm hesitant. I have no real interest in prying into a town's unraveling.

NARRATOR: Amanda Gronich.

AMANDA GRONICH: I've never done anything remotely like this in my life. How do you get people to talk to you? What do you ask?

NARRATOR: Moisés Kaufman.

MOISÉS KAUFMAN: The company has agreed that we should go to Laramie for a week and interview people.

Am a bit afraid about taking ten people in a trip of this nature. Must make some safety rules. No one works alone. Everyone must carry a cell phone. Have made some preliminary contacts with Rebecca Hilliker, head of the theater department at the University of Wyoming. She is hosting a party for us our first night in Laramie and has promised to introduce us to possible interviewees.

MOMENT: REBECCA HILLIKER

REBECCA HILLIKER: I must tell you that when I first heard that you were thinking of coming here, when you first called me, I wanted to say you've just kicked me in the stomach. Why are you doing this to me?

But then I thought, That's stupid, you're not doing this to me. And more importantly, I thought about it and decided that we've had so much negative closure on this whole thing. And the students really need to talk. When this happened they started talking about it, and then the media descended and all dialogue stopped.

You know, I really love my students because they are free thinkers. And you may not like what they have to say, and you may not like their opinions, because they can be very redneck, but they are honest and they're truthful—so there's an excitement here that I never had when I was in the Midwest or in North Dakota, because there, there was so much Puritanism that dictated how people looked at the world that a lot of times they didn't have an opinion, you couldn't get them to express an opinion. And, quite honestly, I'd rather have opinions that I don't like—and have that dynamic in education.

There's a student I think you should talk to. His name is Jedadiah Schultz.

MOMENT: *ANGELS IN AMERICA*

JEDADIAH SCHULTZ: I've lived in Wyoming my whole life. The family has been in Wyoming well . . . for generations. Now when it came time to go to college, my parents can't—couldn't afford to send me to college. I wanted to study theater. And I knew that if I was going to go to college I was going to have to get on a scholarship—and so uh they have this competition each year, this Wyoming state high school competition. And I knew that if I didn't take first place in uh duets that I wasn't gonna get a scholarship. So I went to the theater department of the university looking for good scenes and I asked one of the professors, I was like, "I need—I need a killer scene," and he was like, "Here you go, this is it." And it was from *Angels in America*.

So I read it and I knew that I could win best scene if I did a good enough job.

And when the time came I told my mom and dad so that they would come to the competition. Now you have to understand, my parents go to everything—every ball game, every hockey game—everything I've ever done.

And they brought me into their room and told me that if I did that scene, that they would not come to see me in the competition. Because they believed that it is wrong—that homosexuality is wrong. They felt that strongly about it that they didn't want to come see their son do probably the most important thing he'd done to that point in his life. And I didn't know what to do.

I had never, ever gone against my parents' wishes. But I decided to do it.

And all I can remember about the competition is that when we were done me and my scene partner, we came up to each other and we shook hands and there was a standing ovation.

Oh, man, it was amazing! And we took first place and we won. And that's how come I can afford to be here at the university, because of that scene. It was one of the best moments of my life. And my parents weren't there. And to this day, that was the one thing that my parents didn't see me do.

And thinking back on it, I think, why did I do it? Why did I oppose my parents? 'Cause I'm not gay. So why did I do it? And I guess the only honest answer I can give is that, well *(he chuckles)* I wanted to win. It was such a good scene; it was like the best scene!

Do you know Mr. Kushner? Maybe you can tell him.

MOMENT: JOURNAL ENTRIES

NARRATOR: Company member Greg Pierotti.

GREG PIEROTTI: We arrived today in the Denver Airport and drove to Laramie—

The moment we crossed the Wyoming border I swear I saw a herd of buffalo.

Also, I thought it was strange that the Wyoming sign said:

WYOMING—LIKE NO PLACE ON EARTH instead of
WYOMING—LIKE NO PLACE ELSE ON EARTH.

NARRATOR: Company member Leigh Fondakowski.

LEIGH FONDAKOWSKI: I stopped at a local inn for a bite to eat. And my waitress said to me:

WAITRESS: Hi, my name is Debbie. I was born in nineteen fifty-four and Debbie Reynolds was big then, so yes, there are a lot of us around, but I promise that I won't slap you if you leave your elbows on the table.

MOISÉS KAUFMAN: Today Leigh tried to explain to me to no avail what chicken fried steak was.

WAITRESS: Now, are you from Wyoming? Or are you just passing through?

LEIGH FONDAKOWSKI: We're just passing through.

NARRATOR: Company member Barbara Pitts.

BARBARA PITTS: We arrived in Laramie tonight. Just past the WELCOME TO LARAMIE sign—POPULATION 26,687—the first thing to greet us was Wal-Mart. In the dark, we could be on any main drag in America—fast-food chains, gas stations. But as we drove into the downtown area by the railroad tracks, the buildings still looked like the shape of a turn-of-the-century western town. Oh, and as we passed the University Inn, on the sign where amenities such as heated pool or cable TV are usually touted, it said: HATE IS NOT A LARAMIE VALUE.

NARRATOR: Greg Pierotti.

MOMENT: ALISON AND MARGE

GREG PIEROTTI: I met today with two longtime Laramie residents, Alison Mears and Marge Murray, two social service workers who taught me a thing or two.

ALISON MEARS: Well, what Laramie used to be like when Marge was growing up, well, it was mostly rural.

MARGE MURRAY: Yeah, it was. I enjoyed it, you know. My kids all had horses.

ALISON MEARS: Well, there was more land, I mean, you could keep your pet cow. Your horse. Your little chickens. You know, just have your little bit of acreage.

MARGE MURRAY: Yeah, I could run around the house in my altogethers, do the housework while the kids were in school. And nobody could see me. And if they got that close . . .

ALISON MEARS: Well, then that's their problem.

MARGE MURRAY: Yeah.

GREG PIEROTTI: I just want to make sure I got the expression right: "in your altogethers"?

MARGE MURRAY: Well, yeah, honey, why wear clothes?

ALISON MEARS: Now, how's he gonna use that in his play?

GREG PIEROTTI: So this was a big ranching town?

ALISON MEARS: Oh, not just ranching, this was a big railroad town at one time. Before they moved everything to Cheyenne and Green River and Omaha. So now well, it's just a drive-through spot for the railroad—because even what was it, in the fifties? Well, they had one big roundhouse, and they had such a shop they could build a complete engine.

MARGE MURRAY: They did, my mom worked there.

GREG PIEROTTI: Your mom worked in a roundhouse?

MARGE MURRAY: Yep. She washed engines. Her name was Minnie. We used to, you know, sing that song for her, you know that song.

GREG PIEROTTI: What song?

MARGE MURRAY: "Run for the roundhouse, Minnie, they can't corner you there."
(They crack up.)

ALISON MEARS: But I'll tell you, Wyoming is bad in terms of jobs. I mean, the university has the big high whoop-dee-doo jobs. But Wyoming, unless you're a professional, well, the bulk of the people are working minimum-wage jobs.

MARGE MURRAY: Yeah, I've been either in the service industry or bartending most of my life. Now I know everybody in town.

ALISON MEARS: And she does.

MARGE MURRAY: And I do. Now that I'll tell ya, here in Laramie there is a difference and there always has been. What it is is a class distinction. It's about the well-educated and the ones that are not. And the educated don't understand why the ones that are not don't get educated. That's why I told you before my kids had to fight because their mother was a bartender. Never mind I was the best damn bartender in town.

ALISON MEARS: And she was.

MARGE MURRAY: That's not bragging, that's fact.

ALISON MEARS: But here in Laramie, if it weren't for the university, we'd just be S.O.L.

GREG PIEROTTI: What's S.O.L.?

ALISON MEARS: Well, do I have to say it? Well, it's shit outta luck. *(She cracks up.)* Oh Lordy, you've got that on your tape. Boy, you are getting an education today.

GREG PIEROTTI: Yeah, I guess I am. So, let me just ask you—what was your response when this happened to Matthew Shepard?

MARGE MURRAY: Well, I've been close enough to the case to know many of the people. I have a daughter that's on the Sheriff's Department.

As far as the gay issue, I don't give a damn one way or the other as long as they don't bother me. And even if they did, I'd just say no thank you. And that's the attitude of most of the Laramie population. They might poke one, if they were in a bar situation, you know, they had been drinking, they might actually smack one in the mouth, but then they'd just walk away. Most of 'em said, they would just say, "I don't swing that way" and whistle on about their business. Laramie is live and let live.

ALISON MEARS: I'd say that Marge probably knows a lot more except she's even willing to say and we have to respect her for that.

MARGE MURRAY: Well, uh, where are you going with this story?

GREG PIEROTTI: Oh, well, we still haven't decided. When we've finished, we are going to try to bring it around to Laramie.

MARGE MURRAY: Okay, then, there are parts I won't tell you.

MOMENT: MATTHEW

NARRATOR: Company member Andy Paris.

ANDY PARIS: Today for the first time, we met someone who actually knew Matthew Shepard. Trish Steger, owner of a shop in town, referred to him as Matt.

TRISH STEGER: Matt used to come into my shop—that's how I knew him.

ANDY PARIS: It was the first time I heard him referred to as Matt instead of Matthew. "Did he go by Matt to everyone?"

DOC O'CONNOR: Well, on the second of October, I get a phone call about, uh, ten after seven.

NARRATOR: Doc O'Connor.

DOC O'CONNOR: It was Matthew Shepard. And he said, "Can you pick me up at the corner of Third and Grand?" So, anyhow, I pull up to the corner, to see who Matthew Shepard, you know. It's a little guy, about five-two, soakin' wet, I betcha ninety-seven pounds tops. They say he weighed a hundred and ten, but I wouldn't believe it. They also said he was five-five in the newspapers, but this man, he was really only about five-two, maybe five-one. So he walks up the window—I'm gonna try and go in steps so you can better understand the principle of this man. So he walks up to the window, and I say, "Are you Matthew Shepard?" And he says, "Yeah, I'm Matthew Shepard. But I don't want you to call me Matthew, or Mr. Shepard. I don't want you to call me anything. My name is Matt. And I want you to know, I am gay and we're going to go to a gay bar. Do you have a problem with that?" And I said, "How're you payin'?"

The fact is . . . Laramie doesn't have any gay bars . . . and for that matter neither does Wyoming . . . so he was hiring me to take him to Fort Collins, Colorado, about an hour away.

Matt was a blunt little shit, you know what I'm sayin'?— he always was. But I liked him 'cause he was straightforward, you see what I'm saying? Maybe gay but straightforward, you see what I'm saying?

TRISH STEGER: I don't know, you know, how does any one person ever tell about another? You really should talk to my sister Romaine. She was a very close friend of Matthew's.

ROMAINE PATTERSON: We never called him Matthew, actually, most of the time we called him Choo-choo. You know, because we used to call him Mattchew, and then we just called him Choo-choo.

And whenever I think of Matthew, I always think of his incredible beaming smile. I mean, he'd walk in and he'd be like *(demonstrates)* you know, and he'd smile at everyone . . . he just made you feel great. . . . And he—would like stare people down in the coffee shop . . . 'cause he always wanted to sit on the end seat so that he could talk to me while I was working. And if someone was sitting in that seat, he would just sit there and stare at them. Until they left. And then he would claim his spot.

But Matthew definitely had a political side to him. . . . I mean, he really wanted to get into political affairs . . . that's all his big interest was, was watching CNN and MSNBC, I mean, that's the only TV station I ever saw his TV tuned in to. He was just really smart in political affairs, but not too smart on like commonsense things . . .

So, he moves to Laramie to go to school.

JON PEACOCK: Matthew was very shy when he first came in.

NARRATOR: Jon Peacock, Matthew Shepard's academic advisor.

JON PEACOCK: To the point of being somewhat mousy I'd almost say. He was having some difficulties adjusting, but this was home for him and he made that quite clear. And so his mousiness, his shyness gave way to a person who was excited about this track that he was going to embark on. He was just figuring out wanting to work on human rights, how he was going to do that. And when that happens this person begins to bloom a little bit. He was starting to say, "Wow, there are opportunities here. There are things I can do in this world. I can be important."

ROMAINE PATTERSON: I did hear from Matthew about forty-eight hours before his attack. And he told me that he had joined the gay and lesbian group on campus, and he said he was enjoying it, you know, he was getting ready for Pride Week and whatnot. I mean, he was totally stoked about school—yeah, he was really happy about being there.

JON PEACOCK: And in retrospect, and I can only say this in retrospect of course, I think that's where he was heading, towards human rights. Which only adds to the irony and tragedy of this.

MOMENT: WHO'S GETTING WHAT?

DOC O'CONNOR: Let me tell you something else here. There's more gay people in Wyoming than meets the eye. I know, I know for a fact. They're not particularly, ah, the whattayou call them, the queens, the gay people, queens, you know, runaround faggot-type people. No, they're the ones that throw bales of hay, jump on horses, brand 'em, and kick ass, you see what I'm saying? As I always say, Don't fuck with a Wyoming queer, 'cause they will kick you in your fucking ass, but that's not the point of what I'm trying to say. 'Cause I know a lot of gay people in Wyoming, I know a lot of people period. I've been lived up here some forty-odd years, you see what I'm saying?

And I don't think Wyoming people give a damn one way or another if you're gay or straight, that's just what I just said, doesn't matter. If there's eight men and one woman in a Wyoming bar, which is often the case, now you stop and think—who's getting what? You see what I'm saying? Now jeez, it don't take a big intelligent mind to figure that one out.

MOMENT: EASIER SAID THAN DONE

CATHERINE CONNOLLY: How can I describe what it's really like to be gay here in Laramie?

NARRATOR: Catherine Connolly.

CATHERINE CONNOLLY: I was the first "out" lesbian or gay faculty member on campus. And that was in nineteen ninety-two. Um, I was asked at my interview what my husband did, um, and so I came out then. . . . Do you want a funny story?

When you first get here as a new faculty member, there's all these things you have to do. And so, I was in my office and I noticed that this woman called. . . . I was expecting, you know, it was a health insurance phone call, something like that, and so I called her back. And I could hear her, she's working on her keyboard, clicking away—I said, you know, "This is Cathy Connolly returning your phone call." And she said, "Oh. It's you." And I thought, "This is bizarre." And she said, "I hear—I hear—I hear you're gay. I hear you are." I was like, "Uh huh." And she said, "I hear you came as a couple. I'm one too. Not a couple, just a person." And so—she was—a kind of lesbian who knew I was coming and she wanted to come over and meet me immediately. And she later told me that there were other lesbians that she knew who wouldn't be seen with me. That I would irreparably taint them, that just to be seen with me could be a problem.

I've won almost every teaching award that's possible on campus. And yet even last year, one of my student course evaluations said, "She likes girls. And it shows. She's disgusting."

JONAS SLONAKER: When I came here I knew it was going to be hard as a gay man.

NARRATOR: Jonas Slonaker.

JONAS SLONAKER: I'm not out at work and I've been at my job for four years. And I kept telling myself: People should live where they want to live. And there would be times I would go down to Denver and I would go to gay bars and, um, people would ask where I was from and I'd say, "Laramie, Wyoming." And I met so many men down there from Wyoming. So many gay men who grew up here, and they're like: This is not a place where I can live, how can you live there, I had to

get out, grrr, grrr, grrr. But every once in a while there would
be a guy, "Oh gosh, I miss Laramie. I mean I really love it
there, that's where I want to live." And they get this starry-
eyed look and I'm like: If that's where you want to live, do
it. I mean, imagine if more gay people stayed in small towns.

MOMENT: JOURNAL ENTRIES

MOISÉS KAUFMAN: Today we are moving from our motel and
heading for the Best Western.

NARRATOR: Moisés Kaufman.

MOISÉS KAUFMAN: My hope is that it is a better Western.

NARRATOR: Amanda Gronich.

AMANDA GRONICH: Today we divided up to go to different
churches in the community. Moisés and I were given a Baptist church. We were welcomed into the services by the reverend himself standing at the entrance to the chapel. This is
what I remember of his sermon that morning:

MOMENT: THE WORD

BAPTIST MINISTER: My dear brothers and sisters: I am here today
to bring you the Word of the Lord. Now, I have a simple
truth that I tell to my colleagues and I'm gonna tell it to you
today: The word is either sufficient or it is not.
    Scientists tell me that human history, that the world is
five billion or six billion years old—after all, what's a billion

years give or take. The Bible tells me that human history is six thousand years old.

The word is either sufficient or it is not.

STEPHEN MEAD JOHNSON: Ah, the sociology of religion in the West . . .

NARRATOR: Stephen Mead Johnson, Unitarian minister.

STEPHEN MEAD JOHNSON: Dominant religious traditions in this town: Baptist, Mormon—they're everywhere, it's not just Salt Lake, you know, they're all over—they're like jam on toast down here.

DOUG LAWS: The Mormon Church has a little different thing going that irritates some folks.

NARRATOR: Doug Laws, State Ecclesiastical leader for the Mormon Church.

DOUG LAWS: And that is that we absolutely believe that God still speaks to man. We don't think that it happened and some folks wrote it in the Bible. God speaks to us today. We believe that the prophet of the church has the authority to receive inspiration and revelation from God.

STEPHEN MEAD JOHNSON: So, the spectrum would be—uh, on the left side of that panel: So far left that I am probably sitting by myself, is me—and the Unitarian Church. Unitarians are by and large humanists, many of whom are atheists, I mean—we're, you know, we're not even sure we're a religion. And to my right on the spectrum, to his credit, Father Roger, Catholic priest, who is well-established here, and God bless him—he did not equivocate at all when this happened—he hosted the vigil for Matthew that night.

FATHER ROGER SCHMIT: I was really jolted because you know, when we did the vigil—we wanted to get other ministers involved and we called some of them, and they were not going to get involved. And it was like, "We are gonna stand back and wait and see which way the wind is blowing." And that angered me immensely. We are supposed to stand out as leaders. I thought, "Wow, what's going on here?"

DOUG LAWS: God has set boundaries. And one of our responsibilities is to learn: What is it that God wants? So you study Scripture, you look to your leaders. Then you know what the bounds are. Now once you kinda know what the bounds are, then you sorta get a feel for what's out-of-bounds.

BAPTIST MINISTER: I warn you: You will be mocked! You will be ridiculed for the singularity of your faith! But you let the Bible be your guide. It's in there. It's all in there.

STEPHEN MEAD JOHNSON: The Christian pastors, many of the conservative ones, were silent on this. Conservative Christians use the Bible to show the rest of the world, It says here in the Bible. And most Americans believe, and they do, that the Bible is the word of God, and how you gonna fight that?

BAPTIST MINISTER: I am a Biblicist. Which means: The Bible doesn't need me to be true. The Bible is true whether I believe it or not. The word is either sufficient or it is not.

STEPHEN MEAD JOHNSON: I arrived in Laramie on September fifteenth. I looked around—tumbleweed, cement factory—

and said, "What in the hell am I doing in Wyoming?" Three weeks later, I found out what the hell I'm doing in Wyoming.

MOMENT: A SCARF

STEPHEN BELBER: I had breakfast this morning with a university student named Zubaida Ula. She is an Islamic feminist who likes to do things her own way.

ZUBAIDA ULA: I've lived in Laramie since I was four. Yeah. My parents are from Bangladesh. Two years ago, because I'm Muslim, I decided to start wearing a scarf. That's really changed my life in Laramie. Yeah.

Like people say things to me like "Why do you have to wear that thing on your head?" Like when I go to the grocery store, I'm not looking to give people Islam 101, you know what I mean? So I'll be like, Well, it's part of my religion, and they'll be—this is the worst part 'cause they'll be like, "I know it's part of your religion, but why?" And it's—how am I supposed to go into the whole doctrine of physical modesty and my own spiritual relationship with the Lord, standing there with my pop and chips? You know what I mean?

STEPHEN BELBER: Yeah.

ZUBAIDA ULA: You know, it's so unreal to me that, yeah, that a group from New York would be writing a play about Laramie. And then I was picturing like you're gonna be in a play about my town. You're gonna be onstage in New York and you're gonna be acting like you're us. That's so weird.

MOMENT: LIFESTYLE 1

BAPTIST MINISTER'S WIFE: Hello?

AMANDA GRONICH: Yes, hello. My name is Amanda Gronich and I am here in Laramie working with a theater company. I went to your husband's, the reverend's, your husband's church on Sunday, and I was extremely interested in talking with the reverend about some of his thoughts about recent events.

BAPTIST MINISTER'S WIFE: Well, I don't think he'll want to talk to you. He has very biblical views about homosexuality—he doesn't condone that kind of violence. But he doesn't condone that kind of lifestyle. And he was just bombarded with press after this happened and the media has been just terrible about this whole thing.

AMANDA GRONICH: Oh, I know, I really understand, it must have just been terrible.

BAPTIST MINISTER'S WIFE: Oh, yes, I think we are all hoping this just goes away.

AMANDA GRONICH: Well, um do you think maybe I could call back and speak with your husband just briefly?

BAPTIST MINISTER'S WIFE: Well, all right you can call him back tonight at nine.

AMANDA GRONICH: Oh, thank you so much. I'll do that.

MOMENT: THE FIRESIDE

STEPHEN BELBER: Today Barbara and I went to the Fireside Bar, which is the last place Matthew was seen in public.

BARBARA PITTS: The Fireside—definitely feels like a college bar, with a couple of pool tables and a stage area for karaoke night. Still the few regulars in the late afternoon were hardly the college crowd.

STEPHEN BELBER: First person we talked to was Matt Mickelson, the owner.

MATT MICKELSON: My great-great-grandfather moved here in eighteen sixty-two, he owned Laramie's first opera house, it was called Old Blue Front, and in eighteen seventy Louisa Grandma Swain cast the first woman's ballot in any free election in the world, and that's why Wyoming is the Equality State, so what I want to do is reestablish the Fireside Bar as the Old Blue Front Opera House and Good Time Emporium, you know I want to have a restaurant, a gift shop, a pool hall, and do all this shit, you know . . . every night's ladies' night. . . .

BARBARA PITTS: So, what about the night Matthew Shepard was here?

MATT MICKELSON: We had karaoke that night, twenty or thirty people here—Matthew Shepard came in, sitting right—right where you're sitting, just hanging out. . . . I mean, if you wanna talk to somebody, you should talk to Matt Galloway, he was the kid that was bartending that night. You'd have to meet him, his character stands for itself. *(Calling)* Hey, is Galloway bartending tonight?

MATT GALLOWAY: Okay. I'm gonna make this brief, quick, get it over with, but it will be everything—factual. Just the facts. Here we go. Ten o'clock. I clock in, usual time, Tuesday nights. Ten-thirty—Matthew Shepard shows up—alone—sits down, orders a Heineken.

NARRATOR: Phil Labrie, friend of Matthew Shepard.

PHIL LABRIE: Matt liked to drink Heineken and nothing else. Heineken even though you have to pay nine-fifty for a six-pack. He'd always buy the same beer.

MATT GALLOWAY: So what can I tell you about Matt?

If you had a hundred customers like him it'd be the—the most perfect bar I've ever been in. Okay? And nothing to do with sexual orientation. Um, absolute mannerisms. Manners. Politeness, intelligence.

Taking care of me, as in tips. Everything—conversation, uh, dressed nice, clean-cut. Some people you just know, sits down, "Please," "Thank you"—offers intellect, you know, within—within—within their vocabulary.

Um, so, he kicks it there. Didn't seem to have any worries, or like he was looking for anyone. Just enjoy his drink and the company around.

Now approximately eleven forty-five, eleven-thirty–eleven forty-five, Aaron McKinney and Russell Henderson come in—I didn't know their names then, but they're the accused, they're the perps, they're the accused. They walked in, just very stone-faced, you know. Dirty. Grungy. Rude. "Gimme." That type of thing. They walked up to the bar, uh, and as you know, paid for a pitcher with dimes and quarters, uh, which is something that I mean you don't forget. You don't forget that. Five-fifty in dimes and quarters. That's a freakin' nightmare.

Now Henderson and McKinney, they didn't seem intoxicated at all. They came in—they just ordered a beer, took the pitcher with them back there into the pool room, and kept to themselves. Next thing I knew, probably a half hour later, they were kind of walking around—no beer. And I remember thinking to myself that I'm not gonna ask them if they want another one, because obviously they just paid for a pitcher with dimes and quarters, I have a real good feeling they don't have any more money.

NARRATOR: Romaine Patterson.

ROMAINE PATTERSON: Money meant nothing to Matthew, because he came from a lot of it. And he would like hand over his wallet in two seconds—because money meant nothing. His—shoes—might have meant something. They can say it was robbery . . . I don't buy it. For even an iota of a second.

MATT GALLOWAY: Then a few moments later I looked over and Aaron and Russell had been talking to Matthew Shepard.

KRISTIN PRICE: Aaron said that a guy walked up to him and said that he was gay, and wanted to get with Aaron and Russ.

NARRATOR: Kristin Price, girlfriend of Aaron McKinney.

KRISTIN PRICE: And Aaron got aggravated with it and told him that he was straight and didn't want anything to do with him and walked off. He said that is when he and Russell went to the bathroom and decided to pretend they were gay and get him in the truck and rob him. They wanted to teach him a lesson not to come on to straight people.

MATT GALLOWAY: Okay, no. They stated that Matt approached them, that he came on to them. I absolutely, positively disbelieve and refute the statement one hundred percent. Refute it. I'm gonna give you two reasons why.

One. Character reference.

Why would he approach them? Why them? He wasn't approaching anybody else in the bar. They say he's gay, he was a flaming gay, he's gonna come on to people like that. Bullshit. He never came on to me. Hello?!? He came on to them. I don't believe it.

Two. Territorialism. Is—is—is the word I will use for this. And that's the fact that Matt was sitting there. Russell and Aaron were in the pool area. Upon their first interaction, they were in Matt's area, in the area that Matt had been seen all night. So who approached who by that?

ROMAINE PATTERSON: But Matthew was the kind of person . . . like, he would never not talk to someone for any reason. If someone started talking to him, he'd just be like, "Oh, blah, blah, blah." He never had any problem just striking up a conversation with anybody.

PHIL LABRIE: Matt did feel lonely a lot of times. Me knowing that—and knowing how gullible Matt could be . . . he would have walked right into it. The fact that he was at the bar alone without any friends made him that much more vulnerable.

MATT GALLOWAY: So the only thing is—and this is what I'm testifying to—'cause, you know, I'm also, basically the key eyewitness in this case uh, *(pause)* basically what I'm testifying is that I saw Matthew leave. I saw two individuals leave with

Matthew. I didn't see their faces, but I saw the back of their heads. At the same time, McKinney and Henderson were no longer around. You do the math.

MATT MICKELSON: Actually, I think the DJ was the last one to talk to him on his way out that night . . . gave him a cigarette or something. His name is Shadow.

SHADOW: I was the last person that Matt talked to before he left the Fireside. . . . I was just bullshittin' around with my shit, and he stopped me, I stopped him actually, and he's like "Hey Shadow da da da," and I was like, "What, man, you gettin' ready to leave?" he's like, "Yeah, man, and this an' that." But then I noticed them two guys and they stood outside, you could see, you could see it, they were standing there, you know, and he was looking over to them, and they were lookin' back at him. And I stood and talked to Matt for like a good ten minutes and you seen the guys with him you seen 'em getting like, you seen 'em like worried, like, you know, anxious to leave and shit. . . . So when they took off, I seen it, when they took off, it was in a black truck, it was a small truck, and the three of them sat in the front seat and Matt sat in the middle.

And I didn't think nothin' of it, you know. I didn't figure them guys was gonna be like that?

MOMENT: MCKINNEY AND HENDERSON

NARRATOR: A friend of Aaron McKinney.

ANONYMOUS: Oh, I've known Aaron a long time. Aaron was a good kid, I liked Aaron a lot, that's why I was shocked when I heard this, I'm like . . . I know he was, he was living out far . . . at his trailer house is what he told me, with his girl . . . they just started dating last summer . . . they musta gotten pregnant as soon as they started dating, you know, 'cause they had a kid. He was only twenty-one years old, but he was running around with a kid. . . . You see that's the kinda person Aaron was, just like he always dressed in like big clothes, you know like, in like Tommy "Hile-figer," Polo, Gucci. . . .

At the time I knew him, he was just, he was just a young kid trying to, you know, he just wanted to fit in you know acting tough, acting cool, but you know, you could get in his face about it and he would back down, like he was some kinda scared kid.

NARRATOR: Sherry Aanenson.

SHERRY AANENSON: Russell was just so sweet. He was the one who was the Eagle Scout. I mean his whole presence was just quiet and sweet. And I mean of course it doesn't make sense to me and I know people snap and whatever and like it wasn't a real intimate relationship, I was just his landlord. I did work with him at the Chuck Wagon too. I remember like at the Christmas party at the Chuck Wagon you know? I just saw him and he was just totally drunk out of his mind, like we all were pretty much just party time. . . . And he wasn't belliger-ent, he didn't change, his personality didn't change. He was still the same little meek Russell, I remember him coming up to me and saying, "When you get a chance Sherry can I have a dance?" Which we never did get around to doing that but . . . now I just want to shake him, you know, what were you thinking? What in the hell were you thinking?

MOMENT: THE FENCE

STEPHEN MEAD JOHNSON: The fence—I've been out there four times, I've taken visitors. That place has become a pilgrimage site. Clearly that's a very powerful personal experience to go out there. It is so stark and so empty and you can't help but think of Matthew out there for eighteen hours in nearly freezing temperatures, with that view up there isolated, and, the "God, my God, why have you forsaken me" comes to mind.

NARRATOR: Company member Greg Pierotti.

GREG PIEROTTI: Phil Labrie, a friend of Matthew's, took us to the fence this morning. I broke down the minute I touched it. I feel such a strong kinship with this young man. On the way back, I made sure that no one saw me crying.

NARRATOR: Leigh Fondakowski.

LEIGH FONDAKOWSKI: Greg was crying on the way back. I felt the same way. I have an interview this afternoon with Aaron Kreifels. He's the boy who found Matthew out there at the fence.

MOMENT: FINDING MATTHEW SHEPARD

AARON KREIFELS: Well I, uh, I took off on my bicycle about five P.M. on Wednesday from my dorm. I just kinda felt like going for a ride. So I—I went up to the top of Cactus Canyon, and I'm not super familiar with that area, so on my way back down, I didn't know where I was going, I was just sort of picking the way to go, which now . . . it just makes me think that God wanted me to find him because there's no way that I was going to go that way.

So I was in some deep-ass sand, and I wanted to turn around—but for some reason, I kept going. And, uh, I went along, and there was this rock, on the—on the ground—and I just drilled it. I went—over the handlebars and ended up on the ground.

So, uh, I got up, and I was just kind of dusting myself off, and I was looking around and I noticed something—which ended up to be Matt, and he was just lying there by a fence, and I—I just thought it was a scarecrow. I was like, Halloween's coming up, thought it was a Halloween gag, so I didn't think much of it, so I got my bike, walked it around the fence that was there, it was a buck-type fence. And, uh, got closer to him, and I noticed his hair—and that was a major key to me noticing it was a human being—was his hair. 'Cause I just thought it was a dummy, seriously, I noticed—I even noticed the chest going up and down, I still thought it was a dummy, you know, I thought it was just like some kind of mechanism.

But when I saw hair, well I knew it was a human being.

So . . . I ran to the nearest house and—I just ran as fast as I could . . . and called the police.

OFFICER REGGIE FLUTY: I responded to the call. When I got there, the first—at first the only thing I could see was partially somebody's feet and I got out of my vehicle and raced over—I seen what appeared to be a young man, thirteen, fourteen years old because he was so tiny laying on his back and he was tied to the bottom end of a pole.

I did the best I could. The gentleman that was laying on the ground, Matthew Shepard, he was covered in dry blood all over his head, there was dry blood underneath him and he was barely breathing . . . he was doing the best he could.

I was going to breathe for him and I couldn't get his mouth open—his mouth wouldn't open for me.

He was covered in, like I said, partially dry blood and blood all over his head—the only place that he did not have any blood on him, on his face, was what appeared to be where he had been crying down his face.

His head was distorted, you know, it did not look normal—he looked as if he had a real harsh head wound.

DR. CANTWAY: I was working the emergency room the night Matthew Shepard was brought in. I don't think . . . that any of us, ah, can remember seeing a patient in that condition for a long time—those of us who've worked in big city hospitals have seen this. Ah, but we have some people here who've not worked in a big city hospital. And, ah, it's not something you expect here.

Ah, you expect it, you expect this kind of injuries to come from a car going down a hill at eighty miles an hour. You expect to see gross injuries from something like that—this horrendous, terrible thing. Ah, but you don't expect to see that from someone doing this to another person.

The ambulance report said it was a beating so we knew.

AARON KREIFELS: There was nothing I could do. I mean, if there was anything that I could of done to help him I would've done it but there was nothing.

And I, I was yelling at the top of my lungs at him, trying to get something outta him.

Like: "Hey, wake up," "HELLO!"

But he didn't move, he didn't flinch, he didn't anything . . .

OFFICER REGGIE FLUTY: He was tied to the fence—his hands were thumbs out in what we call a cuffing position—the way we handcuff people. He was bound with a real thin white rope, it went around the bottom of the pole, about four inches up off the ground.

His shoes were missing.

He was tied extremely tight—so I used my boot knife and tried to slip it between the rope and his wrist—I had to be extremely careful not to harm Matthew any further.

DR. CANTWAY: Your first thought is . . . well, certainly you'd like to think that it's somebody from out of town, that comes through and beats somebody. I mean, things like this happen, you know, shit happens, and it happens in Laramie. But if there's been somebody who has been beaten repeatedly, ah, certainly this is something that offends us. I think that's a good word. It offends us!

OFFICER REGGIE FLUTY: He was bound so tight—I finally got the knife through there—I'm sorry—we rolled him over to his left side—when we did that he quit breathing—immediately, I put him back on his back—and that was just enough of an adjustment—it gave me enough room to cut him free there—

I seen the EMS unit trying to get to the location, once the ambulance got there we put a neck collar on him, placed him on a backboard, and scooted him from underneath the fence—then Rob drove the ambulance to Ivinson Hospital's emergency room. . . .

DR. CANTWAY: Now, the strange thing is, twenty minutes before Matthew came in, Aaron McKinney was brought in by his girlfriend. Now I guess he had gotten into a fight later on that night back in town, so I am workin' on Aaron and the ambulance comes in with Matthew. Now at this point I don't know that there's a connection—at all. So I tell Aaron to wait and I go and treat Matthew. So there's Aaron in one room of the ER and Matthew in another room two doors down.

Now as soon as we saw Matthew . . . it was very obvious that his care was beyond our capabilities. Called the neurosurgeon at Poudre Valley Hospital in Fort Collins, Colorado, and he was on the road in an hour and fifteen minutes, I think.

OFFICER REGGIE FLUTY: They showed me a picture . . . days later I saw a picture of Matthew. . . . I would have never recognized him.

DR. CANTWAY: Then two days later I found out the connection and I was . . . very . . . struck!!! They were two kids!!!!! They were both my patients and they were two kids. I took care of both of them. . . . Of both their bodies. And . . . for a brief moment I wondered if this is how God feels when he looks down at us. How we are all his kids. . . . Our bodies. . . . Our souls. . . . And I felt a great deal of compassion. . . . For both of them. . . .

END OF ACT I

ACT II

MOMENT: A LARAMIE MAN

NARRATOR: This is Jon Peacock, Matthew's academic advisor.

JON PEACOCK: Well the news reports started trickling out on Thursday, but no names were mentioned, the brutality of the crime was not mentioned. All that was mentioned was that there was a man, Laramie man found beaten, out on the prairie basically. Later on in the evening they mentioned his name. It was like, That can't, that's not the Matthew Shepard I know, that's not my student, that's not this person who I've been meeting with.

ROMAINE PATTERSON: I was in the coffee shop.

NARRATOR: Romaine Patterson.

ROMAINE PATTERSON: And someone pulled me aside and said, "I don't know much, but they say that there's been a young man who's been beaten in Laramie. And they said his name was Matthew Shepard." And he said, "Do you think this could be our Matthew?"

And I said, "Well, yeah, it sounds like it could be our Matthew."

So I called up my sister Trish and I said, "Tell me what you know." I'm just like—"I need to know anything you know because I don't know anything."

TRISH STEGER: So I'm talking to my sister on the phone and that's when the whole story came up on Channel 5 news and it was just like *ba-boom.*

JON PEACOCK: And the news reports kept rolling in, young University of Wyoming student, his age, his description, it's like, "Oh my God."

TRISH STEGER: And uh I—I felt sick to my stomach . . . it's just instantly sick to my stomach. And I had to tell Romaine, "Yes, it was Matthew. It was your friend."

MATT GALLOWAY: Well, I'll tell you—I'll tell you what is overwhelming.

NARRATOR: Matt Galloway.

MATT GALLOWAY: Friday morning I first find out about it. I go to class, walk out, *boom* there it is—in the *Branding Iron.* So immediately I drive to the nearest newsstand, buy a *Laramie Boomerang* 'cause I want more details, buy that— go home . . . before I can even open the paper, my boss calls me, he says:

MATT MICKELSON: Did you hear about what happened?

MATT GALLOWAY: I'm like, "Yeah."

MATT MICKELSON: Was he in the bar Tuesday night?

MATT GALLOWAY: I go, "Yes, yes he was."

MATT MICKELSON: You've got to get down to the bar right now, we've got to talk about this, we've got to discuss what's going to go on.

JON PEACOCK: By this time, I was starting to get upset, but still the severity wasn't out yet.

RULON STACEY: It was Thursday afternoon.

NARRATOR: Rulon Stacey at Poudre Valley Hospital, Fort Collins, Colorado.

RULON STACEY: I got a call: "We just got a kid in—helicoptered in from Wyoming—and it looks like he may be the victim of a hate crime. We have a couple of newspaper reporters here asking questions." And so, we agreed that we needed one spokesperson: As CEO, I'll do that and we'll try and gather all the information that we can.

ROMAINE PATTERSON: And then I watched the ten o'clock news that night, where they started speaking about the nature and the seriousness of it. . . .

MATT GALLOWAY: So I'm on the phone with Mickelson and he's like:

MATT MICKELSON: We need to go to the arraignment so we can identify these guys, and make sure these guys were in the bar.

MATT GALLOWAY: So we go to the arraignment.

MOMENT: THE ESSENTIAL FACTS

NEWSPERSON: Our focus today turns to Laramie, Wyoming, and the Albany County Courthouse, where Aaron James McKinney and Russell Arthur Henderson are being charged with the brutal beating of Matthew Shepard, a gay University of Wyoming student.

CATHERINE CONNOLLY: The arraignment was on Friday.

NARRATOR: Catherine Connolly.

CATHERINE CONNOLLY: Right around lunchtime. And I said, "I'm just going." I just took off—so I walked a few blocks and I went. Has anybody told you about the arraignment?

There were probably about a hundred people from town and probably as many news media by that point. A lot more of the details had come out. Um, the fact that the perpetrators were kids themselves, local kids, that everyone who's from around here has some relationship to. And what— everyone was really I think waiting on pins and needles for what would happen when the perpetrators walked in. And what happened—there's two hundred people in the room at this point . . . they walked in in their complete orange jumpsuits and their shackles. And, you could have heard a pin drop.

It was incredibly solemn.

I mean, lots of people were teary at that point. Then the judge came in and did a reading—there was a reading of the evidence that the prosecution has and—it's just a—it's a statement of facts, and the reading of the facts was . . .

JUDGE: The essential facts are that the defendants, Aaron James McKinney and Russell Arthur Henderson, met Matthew

Shepard at the Fireside Bar, and after Mr. Shepard confided he was gay, the subjects deceived Mr. Shepard into leaving with them in their vehicle to a remote area. Upon arrival at said area, both subjects tied their victim to a buck fence, robbed him, tortured him, and beat him. . . . Both defendants were later contacted by officers of the Laramie Police Department who observed inside the cab of their pickup, a credit card and a pair of black patent leather shoes belonging to the victim, Matthew Shepard.

(The JUDGE *goes sotto voce here while* CATHERINE CONNOLLY *speaks.)*

The subjects took the victim's credit card, wallet containing cash, his shoes, and other items, and obtained the victim's address in order to later burglarize his home.

CATHERINE CONNOLLY: I don't think there was any person who was left in that courtroom who wasn't crying at the end of it. I mean it lasted—five minutes, but it kept on getting more and more horrific, ending with:

JUDGE: Said defendants left the um, victim begging for his life.

MOMENT: LIVE AND LET LIVE

NARRATOR: Sergeant Hing.

SERGEANT HING: How could this happen? I—I think a lot of people just don't understand, and even I don't really understand, how someone can do something like that. We have one of the most vocal populations of gay people in the state. . . . And it's pretty much: Live and let live.

NARRATOR: Laramie resident Jeffrey Lockwood.

JEFFREY LOCKWOOD: My secret hope was that they were from somewhere else that then of course you can create that distance: We don't grow children like that here. Well, it's pretty clear that we do grow children like that here. . . .

CATHERINE CONNOLLY: So that was the arraignment and my response—was pretty catatonic—not sleeping not eating. Don't—you know, don't leave me alone right now.

JON PEACOCK: More and more details came in about the sheer brutality, um, motivations, how this happened. And then quite frankly the media descended and there was no time to reflect on it anymore.

MOMENT: THE GEM CITY OF THE PLAINS
(Many reporters enter the stage followed by media crews carrying cameras, microphones, and lights. They start speaking into the cameras. Simultaneously, television monitors enter the space—in our production they flew in from above the light grid. In the monitors, one can see in live feed the reporters speaking as well as other media images. The texts overlap to create a kind of media cacophony. This moment should feel like an invasion and should be so perceived by the other actors onstage.)

NEWSPERSON 1: Laramie, Wyoming—often called the "Gem City of the Plains"—is now at the eye of the storm.
(Enter NEWSPERSON 2—NEWSPERSON 1 *goes sotto voce.)*

The cowboy state has its rednecks and yahoos for sure, but there are no more bigots per capita in Wyoming than there are in New York, Florida, or California. The difference is that in

Wyoming there are fewer places to blend in if you're anything other than prairie stock.

NEWSPERSON 2: Aaron McKinney and his friend Russell Henderson came from the poor side of town.
(Enter NEWSPERSON 3—NEWSPERSON 2 *goes sotto voce.)*

Both were from broken homes and as teenagers had had run-ins with the law. They lived in trailer parks and scratched out a living working at fast-food restaurants and fixing roofs.

NEWSPERSON 3: As a gay college student lay hospitalized in critical condition after a severe beating *(enter* NEWSPERSON 4— NEWSPERSON 3 *goes sotto voce)*, this small city, which bills itself as "Wyoming's hometown," wrestled with its attitudes toward gay men.

NEWSPERSON 4: People would like to think that what happened to Matthew was an exception to the rule, but it was an extreme version of what happens in our schools on a daily basis.
(The voices and sounds have escalated to a high pitch. And the last text we hear is:)

NEWSPERSON 1: It's a tough business, as Matt Shepard knew, and as his friends all know, to be gay in cowboy country.
(These reporters continue speaking into the cameras sotto voce over the next texts.)

JON PEACOCK: It was huge. Yeah. It was herds and—and we're talking hundreds of reporters which makes a huge dent in this town's population. There's reporters everywhere, news trucks everywhere on campus, everywhere in the town. And we're not used to that type of attention to begin with, we're not used to that type of exposure.

NARRATOR: Tiffany Edwards, local reporter.

TIFFANY EDWARDS: These people are predators. Like this one journalist actually caught one of the judges in the bathroom at the urinal and was like asking him questions. And the judge was like, "Excuse me, can I please have some privacy?" And the journalist was like *OFFENDED* that he asked for privacy. I mean, this is not how journalism started, like the Gutenberg press, you know.

DOC O'CONNOR: I'll tell you what when *Hard Copy* came and taped me, I taped them at the exact same time. I have every word I ever said on tape so if they ever do anything funny they better watch their fuckin' ass.

NEWSPERSON: Wyoming governor Jim Geringer, a first-term Republican up for reelection.

GOVERNOR GERINGER: I am outraged and sickened by the heinous crime committed on Matthew Shepard. I extend my most heartfelt sympathies to the family.

NEWSPERSON: Governor, you haven't pushed hate crime legislation in the past.

GOVERNOR GERINGER: I would like to urge the people of Wyoming against overreacting in a way that gives one group "special rights over others."

   We will wait and see if the vicious beating and torture of Matthew Shepard was motivated by hate.

SERGEANT HING: You've got the beginning of the news story where they have the graphics in the background, and they've got: "Murder in Wyoming," and Wyoming's dripping red like it's got blood on it or something, and it's like what's the—what is this, this is sensationalism. And . . . we're here going, "Wait a minute. We had the guys in jail in less than a day, I think that's pretty damn good."

EILEEN ENGEN: And for us to be more or less maligned.

NARRATOR: Eileen and Gil Engen.

EILEEN ENGEN: That we're not a good community and we are— The majority of people here are good people.

GIL ENGEN: You git bad apples once in a while. And I think that the gay community took this as an advantage, said this is a good time for us to exploit this.

TIFFANY EDWARDS: Look, I do think that um, the media actually made people accountable. Because people were sitting in their homes, like watching TV and listening to CNN and watching Dan Rather and going, "Jesus Christ, well that's not how it is here." Well how is it here?

NEWSPERSON: Bill McKinney, father of one of the accused.

BILL MCKINNEY: Had this been a heterosexual, these two boys decided to take out and rob, this never would have made the national news. Now my son is guilty before he's even had a trial.

MOMENT: MEDICAL UPDATE

NARRATOR: Rulon Stacey, CEO, Poudre Valley Hospital.

RULON STACEY: By this point, I looked out there and where there had been two or three reporters . . . it must have been another twenty or thirty reporters, ten or fifteen still photographers, and ten video cameras. The parents had just arrived and those poor people . . . I had barely introduced myself to them. I looked out there and I thought, "My gosh. What am I going to do?"

(He crosses to the area where the reporters are gathered with their cameras. As he arrives, several camera flashes go off. He speaks straight into the camera. We see his image on the monitors around the stage.)

NARRATOR: Matthew Shepard medical update at three P.M.
    Saturday, October tenth.

RULON STACEY: Matthew Shepard was admitted in critical condition approximately nine-fifteen P.M., October seventh. When he arrived, he was unresponsive and breathing support was being provided.

Matthew's major injuries upon arrival consisted of hypothermia and a fracture from behind his head to just in front of the right ear. This has caused bleeding in the brain, as well as pressure on the brain. There were also several lacerations on his head, face, and neck.

Matthew's temperature has fluctuated over the last twenty-four hours, ranging from ninety-eight to one hundred and six degrees. We have had difficulty controlling his temperature.

Matthew's parents arrived at seven P.M. October ninth and are now at his bedside. The following is a statement from them:

"First of all, we want to thank the American public for their kind thoughts about Matthew and their fond wishes for his speedy recovery. We appreciate your prayers and goodwill, and we know that they are something Matthew would appreciate, too.

"We also have a special request for the members of the media. Matthew is very much in need of his family at this time, and we ask that you respect our privacy, as well as Matthew's so we can concentrate all of our efforts, thoughts, and love on our son.

"Thank you very much."

MOMENT: SEEING MATTHEW

NARRATOR: Both Aaron McKinney and Russell Henderson pled not guilty to charges. Their girlfriends, Chastity Pasley and Kristin Price also pled not guilty after being charged as accessories after the fact. On our next trip, we spoke to the chief investigating officer on the case, Detective Sergeant Rob DeBree of the Albany County Sheriff's Department.

ROB DEBREE: I guess the thing that bothered me the most was when I went down to Poudre Valley where Matthew was and the thing that bothered me the most is seeing him, touching him, as a homicide detective, you look at bodies. . . . This poor boy is sitting here, fighting all his life, trying to make it. I wanted it so by the book you know.

AARON KREIFELS: I keep seeing that picture in my head when I found him and it's not pleasant whatsoever. I don't want it to be there. I wanna like get it out. That's the biggest part for me is seeing that picture in my head. And it's kind of unbelievable to me you know, that—I happened to be the person who found him—because the big question with me like with my religion, is like, Why did God want ME to find him.

CATHERINE CONNOLLY: I know how to take care of myself, and I was irrationally terrified. So what that means is, not letting my twelve-year-old son walk the streets . . . seeing a truck do a U-turn and thinking it's coming after me. Having to stop because I'm shaking so bad. And in fact, the pickup truck did not come after me, but my reaction was to have my heart in my mouth.

MATT GALLOWAY: Ultimately, no matter how you dice it, I did have an opportunity. If I had—amazing hindsight of 20/20—to have stopped—what occurred . . . and I keep thinkin', "I shoulda noticed. These guys shouldn't a been talking to this guy. I shoulda not had my head down when I was washing dishes for those twenty seconds. Things I coulda done. What the hell was I thinking?"

ROB DEBREE: So you do a lot of studying, you spend hours and hours and hours. You study and study and study . . . talking to the officers, making sure they understand, talk to your witnesses again, and then always coming back to I get this flash of seeing Matthew. . . . I wanted it so tight that there was no way that they were gonna get out of this.

OFFICER REGGIE FLUTY: One of the things that happened when I got to the fence. . . . It was just such an overwhelming amount of blood . . . and we try to wear protective gloves, but we had a really cheap sheriff at the time, and he bought us shit gloves, you know, you put 'em on, you put 'em on, and they kept breaking, so finally you just ran out of gloves, you know. So, you figure, well, you know, "Don't hesitate," you know, that's what your mind tells you all the time: Don't hesitate, and so you just keep moving and you try to help Matthew and find an airway and you know, that's what you do, you know.

MARGE MURRAY: The thing I wasn't telling you before is that Officer Reggie is my daughter. And when she first told me she wanted to be a police officer, well, I thought there was not a better choice for her. She could handle whatever came her way. . . .

OFFICER REGGIE FLUTY: Probably a day and a half later, the hospital called me and told me Matthew had HIV. And the doctor said, "You've been exposed, and you've had a bad exposure," because, you see, I'd been—been building—building a uh, lean-to for my llamas, and my hands had a bunch of open cuts on 'em, so I was kinda screwed, *(she laughs)* you know, and you think, "Oh, shoot," you know.

MARGE MURRAY: Would you like to talk about losing sleep?

OFFICER REGGIE FLUTY: So I said to the doctor, Okay, what do I do? And they said, "Get up here." So, I got up there and we started the ATZ [*sic*] drugs. Immediately.

MARGE MURRAY: Now they told me that's a medication that if it's administered thirty-six hours after you've been exposed . . . it can maybe stop your getting the disease. . . .

OFFICER REGGIE FLUTY: That is a mean nasty medicine. Mean. I've lost ten pounds and a lot of my hair. Yeah. . . .

MARGE MURRAY: And quite frankly I wanted to lash out at somebody. Not at Matthew, please understand that, not one of us was mad at Matthew. But we maybe wanted to squeeze McKinney's head off. And I think about Henderson. And you know two absolutely human beings cause so much grief for so many people. . . . It has been terrible for my whole family, but mostly for her and her kids.

OFFICER REGGIE FLUTY: I think it brought home to my girls what their mom does for a living.

MARGE MURRAY: Well, Reggie, you know what I'm gonna tell you now.

OFFICER REGGIE FLUTY: And my parents . . . told me, you know, they both said the same damn thing.

MARGE MURRAY: You're quitting this damn job!

OFFICER REGGIE FLUTY: And it's just a parent thing, you know, and they're terribly proud of you, 'cause you do a good job whether it's handling a drunk or handling a case like this, but you're you know, they don't want you getting hurt—

MARGE MURRAY: Like I said, there's a right way, a wrong way, and then there's Reggie's way.

OFFICER REGGIE FLUTY: So finally I said, "Oh, for God's sakes, lighten up Francis!"

MARGE MURRAY: You are so stubborn!

OFFICER REGGIE FLUTY: They say I'm stubborn and I don't believe them, but I just think, you know, okay, I've heard your opinion and now here's mine. I'm thirty-nine years old, you know, what are they gonna do, spank me?

MARGE MURRAY: Reggie, don't give me any ideas.

OFFICER REGGIE FLUTY: That would look pretty funny. You know, what can they say?

MARGE MURRAY: I just hope she doesn't go before me. I just couldn't handle that.

MOMENT: E-MAIL

NARRATOR: University of Wyoming president Philip Dubois.

PHILIP DUBOIS: Well, this is a young person—who read my statement on the *Denver Post* story, and sent me an e-mail, to me directly, and said:

E-MAIL SENDER: You and the straight people of Laramie and Wyoming are guilty of the beating of Matthew Shepard just as the Germans who looked the other way are guilty of the deaths of the Jews, the Gypsies, and the homosexuals. You have taught your straight children to hate their gay and lesbian brothers and sisters—unless and until you acknowledge that Matt Shepard's beating is not just a random occurrence, not just the work of a couple of random crazies, you have Matthew's blood on your hands.

PHILIP DUBOIS: And uh, well, I just can't begin to tell you what that does to you. And it's like, you can't possibly know what

I'm thinking, you can't possibly know what this has done to me and my family and my community.

MOMENT: VIGILS

(We see images of the vigils taking place around the country in the monitors as:)

NARRATOR: That first week alone, vigils were held in Laramie, Denver, Fort Collins, and Colorado Springs. Soon after in Detroit, Chicago, San Francisco, Washington, D.C., Atlanta, Nashville, Minneapolis, and Portland, Maine, among others. In Los Angeles, five thousand people gathered, and in New York City, a political rally ended in civil disobedience and hundreds of arrests. And the Poudre Valley Hospital website received close to a million visitors from across the country and around the world, all expressing hope for Matthew's recovery.

MOMENT: MEDICAL UPDATE

NARRATOR: Matthew Shepard medical update at nine A.M.
Sunday, October eleventh.
(RULON STACEY is in front of the cameras. We see him on the monitors.)

RULON STACEY: As of nine A.M. today, Matthew Shepard remains in critical condition.

The family continues to emphasize that the media respect their privacy. The family also wants to thank the American public for their kind thoughts and concern for Matthew.

MOMENT: LIVE AND LET LIVE

JEDADIAH SCHULTZ: There are certain things when I sit in church.

NARRATOR: Jedadiah Schultz.

JEDADIAH SCHULTZ: And the reverend will tell you flat out he doesn't agree with homosexuality—and I don't know—I think right now, I'm still learning about myself and—you know I don't feel like I know enough to make a decision that says, "Homosexuality is right." When you've been raised your whole life that it's wrong—and right now, I would say that I don't agree with it—yeah, that I don't agree with homosexuality but—maybe that's just because I couldn't do it—and speaking in religious terms—I don't think that's how God intended it to happen. But I don't hate homosexuals and I mean—I'm not going to persecute them or anything like that. At all—I mean, that's not gonna be getting in the way between me and the other person at all.

AARON KREIFELS: I'm a Catholic. That's how I was brought up.

NARRATOR: Aaron Kreifels.

AARON KREIFELS: Love the person for who they are, but condemn what they do—condemn the lifestyle. It's like you're almost scared of gay people, for some reason . . . you just have this feeling that . . . you need to be scared. . . . I feel bad that it happened to Matthew Shepard, you know, as a human, but *(pause)* I don't feel like more sympathetic toward the gay community because of it.

CONRAD MILLER: Well, it's preached in schools that being gay is okay.

NARRATOR: Conrad Miller.

CONRAD MILLER: And if my kids asked me, I'd set them down and I'd say, "Well, this is what gay people do. This is what *(scoffs)* animals do. Okay?" And I'd tell 'em, "This is the life, this is the lifestyle, this is what they do." And I'd say, "This is why I believe it's wrong."

MURDOCK COOPER: There's more gay people around than what you think.

NARRATOR: Murdock Cooper.

MURDOCK COOPER: It doesn't bother anybody because most of 'em that are gay or lesbian they know damn well who to talk to. If you step out of line you're asking for it. Some people are saying he made a pass at them. You don't pick up regular people. I'm not excusing their actions but it made me feel better because it was partially Matthew Shepard's fault and partially the guys who did it . . . you know, maybe it's fifty-fifty.

JONAS SLONAKER: Well, there's this whole idea: You leave me alone, I leave you alone.

NARRATOR: Jonas Slonaker.

JONAS SLONAKER: It's in all the western literature, you know, live and let live. Even my gay friends bring it up sometimes. "That is such crap, you know?" Basically what it boils down to: if I don't tell you I'm a fag, you won't beat the crap out of me. I mean, what's so great about that? That's a great philosophy?

ZACKIE SALMON: Yes, as a lesbian I was more concerned for my safety.

NARRATOR: Zackie Salmon.

ZACKIE SALMON: I think we all were. And I think it's because somewhere inside we know it could happen to us anytime, you know. I mean, I would be afraid to walk down the street and display any sort of physical affection for my partner. You don't do that here in Laramie.

MOMENT: IT HAPPENED HERE

ZUBAIDA ULA: We went to the candle vigil.

NARRATOR: Zubaida Ula.

ZUBAIDA ULA: And it was so good to be with people who felt like shit. I kept feeling like I don't deserve to feel this bad, you know? And someone got up there and said uh—he said um, blah blah blah blah blah and then he said, I'm saying it wrong, but basically he said, "C'mon guys, let's show the world that Laramie is not this kind of a town." But it IS that kind of a town. If it wasn't this kind of a town why did this happen here? I mean you know what I mean, like—that's a lie. Because it happened here. So how could it not be a town where this kind of thing happens? Like, that's just totally—like, looking at an Escher painting and getting all confused, like, it's just totally like circular logic like how can you even say that? And we have to mourn this and we have to be sad that we live in a town, a state, a country where shit like this happens. I mean, these are people trying to distance themselves from this crime.

And we need to own this crime. I feel. Everyone needs to own it. We are like this. We ARE like this. WE are LIKE this.

MOMENT: SHANNON AND JEN

STEPHEN BELBER: I was in the Fireside one afternoon and I ran into two friends of Aaron McKinney, Shannon and Jen. *(To* SHANNON *and* JEN*)* You knew Aaron well, right?

SHANNON: Yeah, we both did. When I first found out about this, I thought it was really really awful. I don't know whether Aaron was fucked up or whether he was coming down or what, but Matthew had money. Shit, he had better clothes than I did. Matthew was a little rich bitch.

JEN: You shouldn't call him a rich bitch though, that's not right.

SHANNON: Well, I'm not saying he's a bad guy either, because he was just in the wrong place at the wrong time, said the wrong things. And I don't know, I won't lie to you. There was times that I was all messed up on meth and I thought about going out and robbing. I mean, I never did. But yeah, it was there. It's easy money.

JEN: Aaron's done that thing before. They've both done it. I know one night they went to Cheyenne to go do it and they came back with probably three hundred dollars. I don't know if they ever chose like gay people as their particular targets before, but anyone that looked like they had a lot of money and that was you know, they could outnumber, or overpower, was fair game.

STEPHEN BELBER: But do you think there was any homophobia involved in this that contributed to some of it?

JEN: Probably. It probably would've pissed him off that Matthew was gay 'cause he didn't like—the gay people I've seen him interact with, he was fine as long as, you know, they didn't hit on him. As long as it didn't come up.

SHANNON: Yeah, as long as they weren't doing it in front of him.

STEPHEN BELBER: Do you get the impression that Aaron knew other gay people?

SHANNON: I'm sure that he knew people that are gay. I mean, he worked up at KFC and there was a couple people up there that—yeah *(he laughs)*—and I'm not saying it's bad or anything 'cause I don't know, half the people I know in Laramie are gay.

STEPHEN BELBER: What would you guys say to Aaron if you saw him right now?

SHANNON: First of all, I'd ask him if he'd ever do any more tweak.

JEN: He wouldn't I bet. If I saw Aaron now, I'd be like, "Man, why'd you fuck up like that?" But, I'd want to make sure he's doing good in there. But, I'm sure he is though. I'd probably just want to like hang out with him.

SHANNON: Smoke a bowl with him.

JEN: I bet he wants one so bad.

STEPHEN BELBER: So, you guys both went to Laramie High?

SHANNON: Yeah. Can't you tell? We're a product of our society.

MOMENT: HOMECOMING

NEWSPERSON: On a day that is traditionally given over to nothing more profound than collegiate exuberance and the fortunes of the University of Wyoming football team, this community on the high plains had a different kind of homecoming Saturday, as many searched their souls in the wake of a vicious, apparent antigay hate crime.

NARRATOR: University president Philip Dubois.

PHILIP DUBOIS: This was homecoming weekend. There were a lot of people in town, and there's a homecoming parade that was scheduled and then the students organized to tag onto the back of it—you know, behind the banner supporting Matt, and everybody wearing the armbands that the students had created. . . .

HARRY WOODS: I live in the center of town.

NARRATOR: Harry Woods.

HARRY WOODS: And my apartment has windows on two opposite streets. One goes north and one goes south. And that is exactly the homecoming parade route. Now, on the day of the parade, I had a cast on my leg because of a fall. So I was very disappointed because I really wanted to walk with the people that were marching for Matthew. But I couldn't. So I watched from my window. And it was . . . it was just . . . I'm fifty-two years old and I'm gay. I have lived here for many years and I've seen a lot. And I was very moved when I saw the tag on the end of the homecoming parade. About a hundred people walking behind a banner for Matthew Shepard.

So then the parade went down to the end of the block to make a U-turn, and I went to the other side of my apartment to wait for it to come south down the other street.

MATT GALLOWAY: I was right up in front there where they were holding the banner for Matthew, and let me tell you . . . I've never had goose bumps so long in my life. It was incredible. A mass of people. Families—mothers holding their six-year-old kids, tying these armbands around these six-year-old kids and trying to explain to them why they should wear an armband. Just amazing. I mean it was absolutely one of the most—beautiful things I've ever done in my life.

HARRY WOODS: Well, about ten minutes went by and sure enough the parade started coming down the street. And then I noticed the most incredible thing . . . as the parade came down the street . . . the number of people walking for Matthew Shepard had grown five times. There were at least five hundred people marching for Matthew. Five hundred people. Can you imagine? The tag at the end was larger than the entire parade. And people kept joining in. And you know what? I started to cry. Tears were streaming down my face. And I thought: Thank God that I got to see this in my lifetime. And my second thought was, "Thank you, Matthew."

MOMENT: ONE OF OURS

SHERRY JOHNSON: I really haven't been all that involved, per se. My husband's a highway patrolman, so that's really the only way that I've known about it.

Now when I first found out I just thought it was horrible. I just, I can't. . . . Nobody deserves that! I don't care who ya are.

But, the other thing that was not brought out—at the same time this happened that patrolman was killed. And there was nothing. Nothing. They didn't say anything about the old man that killed him. He was driving down the road and he shouldn't have been driving and killed him. It was just a little piece in the paper. And we lost one of our guys.

You know, my husband worked with him. This man was brand-new on the force. But, I mean, here's one of ours, and it was just a little piece in the paper.

And a lot of it is my feeling that the media is portraying him as a saint. And making him as a martyr. And I don't think he was. I don't think he was that pure.

Now, I didn't know him, but . . . there's just so many things about him that I found out that I just, it's scary. You know about his character and spreading AIDS and a few other things, you know, being the kind of person that he was. He was, he was just a barfly, you know. And I think he pushed himself around. I think he flaunted it.

Everybody's got problems. But why they exemplified him I don't know. What's the difference if you're gay? A hate crime is a hate crime. If you murder somebody you hate 'em. It has nothing to do with if you're gay or a prostitute or whatever.

I don't understand. I don't understand.

MOMENT: TWO QUEERS AND A CATHOLIC PRIEST

NARRATOR: Company member Leigh Fondakowski.

LEIGH FONDAKOWSKI: This is one of the last days on our second trip to Laramie. Greg and I have been conducting interviews nonstop and we are exhausted.

GREG PIEROTTI: We are to meet Father Roger at seven-thirty in the morning. I was wishing we could skip it altogether, but here we go: seven-thirty A.M., two queers and a Catholic priest.

FATHER ROGER SCHMIT: Matthew Shepard has served us well. You realize that? He has served us well. And I do not mean to condemn Matthew to perfection, but I cannot mention anyone who has done more for this community than Matthew Shepard.

And I'm not gonna sit here and say, "I was just this bold guy—no fear." I was scared—I was very vocal in this community when this happened—and I thought, "You know, should we, uh, should we call the bishop and ask him permission to do the vigil?" And I was like, "Hell, no, I'm not going to do that." His permission doesn't make it correct, you realize that? And I'm not knocking bishops, but what is correct is correct.

You people are just out here on a search though. I will do this, I will trust you people that if you write a play of this, that you *(pause)* say it right, say it correct. I think you have a responsibility to do that.

Don't—don't—don't um, *(pause)* don't make matters worse. . . . You think violence is what they did to Matthew— they did do violence to Matthew—but you know, every time that you are called a fag, or you are called a you know, a lez or whatever . . .

LEIGH FONDAKOWSKI: Or a dyke.

FATHER ROGER SCHMIT: Dyke! Yeah, dyke! Do you realize that is violence? That is the seed of violence. And I would resent it immensely if you use anything I said, uh, you know, to—to somehow cultivate that kind of violence, even in its smallest form—I would resent it immensely. You need to know that.

LEIGH FONDAKOWSKI: Thank you, Father, for saying that.

FATHER ROGER SCHMIT: Just deal with what is true. You know what is true. You need to do your best to say it correct.

MOMENT: CHRISTMAS

NARRATOR: Andrew Gomez.

ANDREW GOMEZ: I was in there, I was in jail with Aaron in December. I got thrown in over Christmas. Assault and battery, two counts. I don't wanna talk about it. But we were sittin' there eatin' our Christmas dinner, tryin' to eat my stuffing, my motherfucking bread, my little roll and whatnot, and I asked him, I was like, "Hey, homey, tell me something, tell me something please, why did you—" Okay I'm thinking how I worded this, I was like, "Why did you KILL a faggot if you're gonna be destined to BE a faggot later?" You know? I mean think about it, he's either gonna get humped a lot or he's gonna die. So why would you do that, think about that. I don't understand that.

And you know what he told me? Honest to God, this is what he said, he goes: "He tried to grab my dick." That's what he said, man! He's dumb, dog, he don't even act like it was nothin'.

Now I heard they was auctioning those boys off. Up there in the max ward, you know, where the killers go, I heard that when they found out Aaron was coming to prison, they were auctioning those boys off. "I want him. I'll put aside five, six, seven cartons of cigarettes." Auction his ass off. I'd be scared to go to prison if I was those two boys.

MOMENT: LIFESTYLE 2

BAPTIST MINISTER: Hello.

AMANDA GRONICH: Reverend?

BAPTIST MINISTER: Yes, hello.

AMANDA GRONICH: I believe your wife told you a bit about why I'm contacting you.

BAPTIST MINISTER: Yes, she did. And let me tell you—uh—I don't know that I really want to talk to anyone about any of this incident—uh—I am somewhat involved and I just don't think—

AMANDA GRONICH: Yes, I completely understand and I don't blame you. You know, I went to your service on Sunday.

BAPTIST MINISTER: You went to the services on Sunday?

AMANDA GRONICH: Yes, I did.

BAPTIST MINISTER: Did I meet you?

AMANDA GRONICH: Yes, you welcomed me at the beginning, I believe.

BAPTIST MINISTER: I see. Well, let me tell you. I am not afraid to be controversial or to speak my mind, and that is not necessarily the views of my congregation per se. Now as I said, I am somewhat involved—that half the people in the case—well, the girlfriend of the accused, Kristen Price, is a member of our congregation, and one of the accused, Aaron McKinney, has visited.

AMANDA GRONICH: Mmmmmm.

BAPTIST MINISTER: Now, those two people, the accused, have forfeited their lives. We've been after the two I mentioned for ages, trying to get them to live right, to do right. Now, one boy is on suicide watch and I am working with him—until they put him in the chair and turn on the juice I will work for his salvation. Now I think they deserve the death penalty—I will try to deal with them spiritually.

AMANDA GRONICH: Right, I understand.

BAPTIST MINISTER: Now, as for the victim, I know that that lifestyle is legal, but I will tell you one thing: I hope that Matthew Shepard as he was tied to that fence that he had time to reflect on a moment when someone had spoken the word of the Lord to him—and that before he slipped into a coma he had a chance to reflect on his lifestyle.

AMANDA GRONICH: Thank you, Reverend, I appreciate your speaking with me.
(Rain begins to fall on the stage.)

MOMENT: THAT NIGHT

RULON STACEY: About eleven-thirty that night, I had just barely gone to bed, and Margo our chief operating officer called and said, "His blood pressure has started to drop." "Well, let's wait and see." She called me about ten after—he just died. So I quick got dressed and came in. And uh, and went into the ICU where the family was, and Judy came up and she put her arms around me and I put my arms around her and we just stood there—honestly, for about ten minutes just—'cause what else do you do?

And then we had to sit and talk about things that you just— "Dennis, it's now public knowledge. . . . And I'm gonna go out there now and tell the whole world that this has happened."

'Cause by this point it was clear to us that it was the world—it was the whole world.

And so Judy told me what she wanted me to say. And I went out at four A.M.

(He crosses to the camera.)

MOMENT: MEDICAL UPDATE

NARRATOR: Matthew Shepard medical update for four-thirty A.M. Monday, October twelfth.

RULON STACEY: At twelve midnight on Monday, October twelfth, Matthew Shepard's blood pressure began to drop. We immediately notified his family, who were already at the hospital.

At twelve fifty-three A.M. Matthew Shepard died. His family was at his bedside.

The family did release the following statement:

"The family again asked me to express their sincerest gratitude to the entire world for the overwhelming response for their son.

"The family was grateful that they did not have to make a decision regarding whether or not to continue life support for their son. Like a good son, he was caring to the end and removed guilt or stress from the family.

"He came into the world premature and left the world premature."

Matthew's mother said, "Go home, give your kids a hug, and don't let a day go by without telling them that you love them."

MOMENT: MAGNITUDE

RULON STACEY: And—I don't know *how* I let that happen—I lost it on national television, but, you now, we had been up for like seventy-two hours straight and gone home and gone to sleep for half an hour and had to get up and come in— and maybe I was just way—I don't know—but, *(pause)* in a moment of complete brain-deadness, while I was out there reading that statement I thought about my own four daughters—and go home hug your kids *(he begins to cry)* and oh, she doesn't have her kid anymore.

And there I am and I'm thinking "This is so lame."

Um, and then we started to get people sending us e-mails and letters. And most of them were just generally very kind. But I did get this one. This guy wrote me and said, "Do you cry like a baby on TV for all of your patients or just the faggots?" And as I told you before, homosexuality is not a lifestyle with which I agree. Um, but having been thrown into this *(pause)* I guess I didn't understand the magnitude with which some people hate. And of all the letters that we got, there were maybe two or three that were like that, most of them were, Thank you for your caring and compassion, and Matthew had caring and compassion from the moment he got here.

MOMENT: H-O-P-E

STEPHEN BELBER: I spoke with Doc today and told him we would soon be coming back out for the upcoming trials of Russell Henderson and Aaron McKinney, and this is what he had to say:

DOC O'CONNOR: I'll tell you what, if they put those two boys to death, that would defeat everything Matt would be thinking about on them. Because Matt would not want those two to die. He'd want to leave them with hope. *(Spelling)* H-O-P-E. Just like the whole world hoped that Matt would survive. The whole thing, you see, the whole thing, ropes around hope, H-O-P-E.

END OF ACT II

ACT III

(The stage is now empty except for several chairs stage right. They occupy that half of the stage. They are all facing the audience and arranged in rows as if to suggest a church or a courthouse. As the lights come up, several actors are sitting there dressed in black. Some of them have umbrellas. A few beats with just this image in silence. Then MATT GALLOWAY *enters stage left. Looks at them and says:)*

MOMENT: SNOW

MATT GALLOWAY: The day of the funeral, it was snowing so bad, big huge wet snowflakes. And when I got there, there were thousands of people in just black, with umbrellas everywhere. And there were two churches—one for the immediate family uh, invited guests, people of that nature, and then one church for everybody else who wanted to be there. And then still, hundreds of people outside that couldn't fit into either of the churches. And there was a big park by the church, and that's where these people were. And this park was full.

PRIEST: The liturgy today is an Easter liturgy. It finds its meaning in the Resurrection. The service invites your full participation. The Lord be with you.

PEOPLE: And also with you.

PRIEST: Let us pray.

TIFFANY EDWARDS: And I guess it was like the worst storm that they have had.

NARRATOR: Tiffany Edwards.

TIFFANY EDWARDS: Like that anybody could ever tell, like trees fell down and the power went out for a couple of days because of it and I just thought, "It's like the forces of the universe at work, you know." Whatever higher spirit you know, is like that blows storms, was blowin' this storm.

PRIEST: For our brother, Matthew, let us pray to our Lord Jesus Christ who said, "I am the Resurrection and the Life." We pray to the Lord.

PEOPLE: HEAR US, LORD.
(The PRIEST *begins prayers and goes into sotto voce.)*

PRIEST: Lord, you who consoled Martha and Mary in their distress: draw near to us who mourn for Matthew, and dry the tears of those who weep. We pray to the Lord.

PEOPLE: HEAR US, LORD.

PRIEST: You wept at the grave of Lazarus, your friend; comfort us in our sorrow. We pray to the Lord.

PEOPLE: HEAR US, LORD.

PRIEST: You raised the dead to life; give to our brother eternal life. We pray to the Lord.

PEOPLE: HEAR US, LORD.

PRIEST: You promised paradise to the thief who repented; bring our brother the joys of heaven. We pray to the Lord.

PEOPLE: HEAR US, LORD.

PRIEST: He was nourished with your Body and Blood; grant him a place at the table in your heavenly kingdom. We pray to the Lord.

PEOPLE: HEAR US, LORD.

PRIEST: Comfort us in our sorrows at the death of our brother; let our faith be our consolation, and eternal life our hope. We pray to the Lord.

KERRY DRAKE: My most striking memory from the funeral.

NARRATOR: Kerry Drake, *Casper Star-Tribune.*

KERRY DRAKE: Is seeing the Reverend Fred Phelps from Kansas . . . that scene go up in the park.

REVEREND FRED PHELPS: Do you believe the Bible? Do you believe you're supposed to separate the precious from the vile? You don't believe that part of the Bible? You stand over there ignorant of the fact that the Bible—two times

for every verse it talks about God's love it talks about God's hate.
(REVEREND FRED PHELPS *continues sotto voce.*)

KERRY DRAKE: A bunch of high school kids who got out early came over and started yelling at some of these people in the protest—the Fred Phelps people, and across the street you had people lining up for the funeral. . . . Well, I remember a guy, this skinhead coming over and he was dressed in leather and spikes everywhere and he came over from across the street where the protest was and I just thought, Oh, this is gonna be a really ugly confrontation, but he came over and he started leading them in "Amazing Grace."
(*The people sing "Amazing Grace."*)

REVEREND FRED PHELPS: We wouldn't be here if this was just another murder the state was gonna deal with. The state deals with hundreds of murders every single day. But this murder is different, because the fags are bringing us out here trying to make Matthew Shepard into a poster boy for the gay lifestyle. And we're going to answer it. It's just that simple.
(REVEREND FRED PHELPS *continues sotto voce.*)

NARRATOR: Six months later, the company returned to Laramie for the trial of Russell Henderson, the first of the two per-petrators. It was to be a capital murder trial. When we got to the Albany County Courthouse, Fred Phelps was already there.

REVEREND FRED PHELPS: You don't like that attribute of God.

NARRATOR: But so was Romaine Patterson.

REVEREND FRED PHELPS: That perfect attribute of God. Well, *we* love that attribute of God and we're going to preach it. Because God's hatred is pure. It's a determination—it's a determination that he's gonna send some people to hell. That's God's hatred. . . .
(Continues sotto voce.)

We're standing here with God's message. We're standing here with God's message. Is homosexuality—is being a fag okay? What do you mean it's not for you to judge? If God doesn't hate fags, why does he put 'em in hell? . . . You see the barrenness and sterility of your silly arguments when set over against some solid gospel truth? Barren and sterile. Like your lifestyle. Your silly arguments.

ROMAINE PATTERSON: After seeing Fred Phelps protesting at Matthew's funeral and finding out that he was coming to Laramie for the trial of Russell Henderson, I decided that someone needed to stand toe-to-toe with this guy and show the differences. And I think at times like this when we're talking about hatred as much as the nation is right now, that someone needs to show . . . that there is a better way of dealing with that kind of hatred.

So our idea is to dress up like angels. And so we have designed an angel outfit—for our wings are HUGE—they're like big-ass wings—and there'll be ten to twenty of us that are angels—and what we're gonna do is we're gonna encircle Phelps . . . and because of our big wings—we are gonna com-plete-ly block him.

So this big-ass band of angels comes in, we don't say a fuckin' word, we just turn our backs to him and we stand there. . . . And we are a group of people bringing forth a message of peace and love and compassion. And we're calling it "Angel Action."

Yeah, this twenty-one-year-old little lesbian is ready to walk the line with him.

REVEREND FRED PHELPS: When those old preachers laid their hands on me it's called an ordination. Then they deliver a charge. Mine was from Isaiah fifty-eight: one—"Cry aloud. Spare not. Lift up thy voice like a trumpet and show my people their transgressions."

ROMAINE PATTERSON: And I knew that my angels were gonna be taking the brunt of everything he had to yell and say. I mean, we were gonna be blocking his view and he was gonna be liked pissed off to all hell. . . . So I went out and bought all my angels earplugs.
("Amazing Grace" ends.)

MOMENT: JURY SELECTION

BAILIFF: The court is in session.
(All stand.)

NARRATOR: Romaine Patterson's sister, Trish Steger.

TRISH STEGER: As soon as they started jury selection, you know, everybody was coming into my shop with "I don't want to be on this trial. I hope they don't call me." Or, "Oh my God, I've been called. How do I get off?" Just wanting to get as far away from it as they could . . . very fearful that they were going to have to be part of that jury.

And then I heard . . . Henderson had to sit in the courtroom while they questioned the prospective jurors. And one of the questions that they ask is: Would you be willing to put this person to death?

And I understand that a lot of the comments were:

JUROR: Yes, I would, Your Honor.

JUROR: Yes, sir.

JUROR: Absolutely.

JUROR: Yes, sir!
(*Jurors continue underneath.*)

JUROR: No problem.

JUROR: Yep.

TRISH STEGER: These are people he grew up with. Can you imagine hearing that? You know, juror after juror after juror . . .

MOMENT: RUSSELL HENDERSON
(*"Amazing Grace" begins again.*)

JUDGE: You entered a not guilty plea earlier, Mr. Henderson. But I understand you wish to change your plea today; is that correct?

RUSSELL HENDERSON: Yes, sir.

JUDGE: You understand, Mr. Henderson, that the recommended sentence here is two life sentences?

RUSSELL HENDERSON: Yes, sir.

JUDGE: Do you understand that those may run concurrently or they may run consecutively?

RUSSELL HENDERSON: Yes, sir.

JUDGE: Mr. Henderson, I will now ask you how you wish to plead, guilty or not guilty?

RUSSELL HENDERSON: Guilty.

JUDGE: Before the Court decides whether the sentences will be concurrent or consecutive, I understand that there are statements to be made by at least one individual.

NARRATOR: This is an excerpt from a statement made to the court by Lucy Thompson.

LUCY THOMPSON: As the grandmother and the person who raised Russell, along with my family, we have written the following statement: Our hearts ache for the pain and suffering that the Shepards have went through. We have prayed for your family since the very beginning. Many times throughout the day I have thought about Matt. And you will continue to be in our thoughts and prayers, as we know that your pain will never go away. You have showed such mercy in allowing us to have this plea, and we are so grateful that you are giving us all the opportunity to live. Your Honor, we, as a family, hope that as you sentence Russell, that you will do it concurrently two life terms. For the Russell we know and love, we humbly plead, Your Honor, to not take Russell completely out of our lives forever.

JUDGE: Thank you. Mr. Henderson, you have a constitutional right to make a statement. Do you have anything you would like to say?

RUSSELL HENDERSON: Yes, I would, Your Honor. Mr. and Mrs. Shepard, there is not a moment that goes by that I don't see what happened that night. I know what I did was very wrong, and I regret greatly what I did. You have my greatest sympathy for what happened. I hope that one day you will be able to find it in your hearts to forgive me. Your Honor, I know what I did was wrong. I'm very sorry for what I did, and I'm ready to pay my debt for what I did.

JUDGE: Mr. Henderson, you drove the vehicle that took Matthew Shepard to his death. You bound him to that fence in order that he might be more savagely beaten and in order that he might not escape to tell his tale. You left him out there for eighteen hours, knowing full well that he was there, perhaps having an opportunity to save his life, and you did nothing. Mr. Henderson, this Court does not believe that you really feel any true remorse for your part in this matter. And I wonder, Mr. Henderson, whether you fully realize the gravity of what you've done.

The Court finds it appropriate, therefore, that sentence be ordered as follows: As to Count Three, that being felony murder with robbery, you are to serve a period of imprisonment for the term of your natural life. On Count One, kidnapping, that you serve a period of imprisonment for the term of your natural life. Sentencing for Count One to run consecutive to sentencing for Count Three.

NARRATOR: After the hearing, we spoke with Gene Pratt, Russell Henderson's Mormon home teacher.

GENE PRATT: I've known Russell's family for thirty-eight years. Russell's only twenty-one so I've known him his entire life. I ordained Russell a priest of the Mormon Church, so when this happened, you can imagine—disbelief. . . . After the sentencing . . . the church held a disciplinary council and the result of that meeting was to excommunicate Russell from the Mormon Church. So what that means is that your name is taken off the records of the church. So nobody's assigned to visit you, you won't remember that person when you are praying, you don't bring their name up in a certain context. So you just disappear.

Russell's reaction to that was not positive, it hurt him, and it hurt him too to realize how serious a transgression he had committed.

But I will not desert Russell. That's a matter of my religion and my friendship with the family.

(All exit. Lights fade on RUSSELL, *his grandmother, and his home teacher.)*

MOMENT: *ANGELS IN AMERICA*

NARRATOR: Before we left Laramie, we met again with Rebecca Hilliker at the theater department. She is producing *Angels in America* this year at the university.

REBECCA HILLIKER: I think that's the focus the university has taken—is that we have a lot of work to do. That we have an obligation to find ways to reach our students. . . . And the question is—how do we move—how do we reach a whole state where there is some really deep-seated hostility toward gays. How do you reach them?

This is the beginning . . . and guess who's auditioning for the lead?

JEDADIAH SCHULTZ: MY PARENTS!

NARRATOR: Jedadiah Schultz.

JEDADIAH SCHULTZ: My parents were like, So what plays are you doing this year at school. And I was like, *Angels in America* and I told them the whole list of plays. And they're like, *Angels in America?* Is that . . . that play you did in high school? That scene you did in high school? And I was like: Yeah. And she goes: Huh. So are you gonna audition for it? And I was like yeah. And we got in this huge argument . . . and my best, the best thing that I knew I had them on is it was just after they had seen me in a performance of *Macbeth* and onstage like I murdered like a little kid, and Lady Macduff and these two other guys and like and she goes well, you know homosexuality is a sin—she kept saying that—and I go, Mom, I just played a murderer tonight. And you didn't seem to have a problem with that. . . ."

I tell you. I've never prepared myself this much for an audition in my life. Never ever. Not even close.

ROB DEBREE: Not having to deal that much with the gay society here in Laramie.

NARRATOR: Detective Sergeant Rob DeBree.

ROB DEBREE: Well, once we started working into the case, and actually speaking to the people that were gay and finding out what their underlying fears were, well, then it sort of hit home. This is America. You don't have the right to feel that fear.

And we're still going to have people who hold with the old ideals, and I was probably one of them fourteen months ago. I'm not gonna put up with it, and I'm not going to listen to it. And if they don't like my views on it, fine. The door goes both ways. I already lost a couple of buddies. I don't care. I feel more comfortable and I can sleep at night.

OFFICER REGGIE FLUTY: Well, you're tested every three months.

NARRATOR: Officer Reggie Fluty.

OFFICER REGGIE FLUTY: And I was able to have the DNA test done. And so they got me to Fort Collins, they drew the blood there, flew it to Michigan, and did all the DNA work there and—which was—a week later . . . I knew I was negative for good.

MARGE MURRAY: I'll tell ya, we were all on our knees saying Hail Marys.

OFFICER REGGIE FLUTY: You were just elated, you know, and you think, "Thank God!"

MARGE MURRAY: So what's the first thing she does?

OFFICER REGGIE FLUTY: I stuck my tongue right in my husband's mouth. I was just happy, you know, you're just so happy. You think, "Yeah, I hope I did this service well," you know, I hope I did it with some kind of integrity. And my daughters just bawled.

MARGE MURRAY: They were so happy.

OFFICER REGGIE FLUTY: And the force . . .

MARGE MURRAY: Oh boy . . .

OFFICER REGGIE FLUTY: We went out and got shitfaced.

MARGE MURRAY: *(Simultaneous)* Shitfaced.

OFFICER REGGIE FLUTY: They all bought me drinks too, it was great . . . and everybody hugged and cried and, you know, I kissed everybody who walked through the door. . . .

MARGE MURRAY: Reggie, they don't need to know that.

OFFICER REGGIE FLUTY: I didn't care if they were male or female, they each got a kiss on the lips.
(REGGIE *and* MARGE *exit together, arguing as they go.)*

MARGE MURRAY: Now what part of what I just said didn't you understand?

OFFICER REGGIE FLUTY: Oh, get over it, Maw!

MOMENT: A DEATH PENALTY CASE

NARRATOR: Almost a year to the day that Matthew Shepard died, the trial for Aaron James McKinney was set to begin.

CAL RERUCHA: Probably the question that most of you have in your mind is ah, ah, how the McKinney case will proceed.

NARRATOR: Cal Rerucha, prosecuting attorney.

CAL RERUCHA: And it's the decision of the county attorney's office that that will definitely be a death penalty case.

MARGE MURRAY: Part of me wants McKinney to get it. But I'm not very proud of that. I was on and off, off and on. I can't say what I would do. . . . I'm too personally involved.

ZACKIE SALMON: Oh, I believe in the death penalty one hundred percent. You know, because I want to make sure that guy's ass dies. This is one instance where I truly believe with all my heart an eye for an eye a tooth for a tooth.

MATT MICKELSON: I don't know about the death penalty. But I don't ever want to see them ever walk out of Rawlins Penitentiary. I'll pay my nickel, or whatever, my little percentage of tax, nickel a day to make sure that his ass stays in there and never sees society again and definitely never comes into my bar again.

MATT GALLOWAY: I don't believe in the death penalty. It's too much for me. I don't believe that one person should be killed as redemption for his having killed another. Two wrongs don't make a right.

ZUBAIDA ULA: How can I protest, if the Shepards want McKinney dead? I just can't interfere in that. But on a personal level, I knew Aaron in grade school. We never called him Aaron, he was called A.J. . . . How can we put A.J. McKinney, how can we put A.J. McKinney to death?

FATHER ROGER SCHMIT: I think right now our most important teachers must be Russell Henderson and Aaron McKinney. They have to be our teachers. How did you learn? What did we as a society do to teach you that? See I don't know if many people will let them be their teachers. I think it would be wonderful if the judge said, In addition to your sentence: you must tell your story, you must tell your story.

BAILIFF: All rise. State of Wyoming versus Aaron James McKinney docket number 6381. The Honorable Barton R. Voigt presiding. The Court is in session.

MOMENT: AARON MCKINNEY

NARRATOR: During the trial of Aaron McKinney, the prosecution played a tape recording of his confession.

ROB DEBREE: My name is Rob DeBree, sergeant for the Sheriff's Office. You have the right to remain silent. Anything you say can and may be used against you in the court of law.

NARRATOR: The following is an excerpt of that confession.

ROB DEBREE: Okay, so you guys, you and Russ go to the Fireside. So you're at the Fireside by yourselves, right?

AARON MCKINNEY: Yeah.

ROB DEBREE: Okay, where do you go after you leave the Fireside?

AARON MCKINNEY: Some kid wanted a ride home.

ROB DEBREE: What's he look like?

AARON MCKINNEY: Mmm, like a queer. Such a queer dude.

ROB DEBREE: He looks like a queer?

AARON MCKINNEY: Yeah, like a fag, you know?

ROB DEBREE: Okay. How did you meet him?

AARON MCKINNEY: The fag? The queer guy? We were meeting at the bar. He asked us what we were drinkin', what we were doin'.

ROB DEBREE: Okay. Tell me what happened after you met him?

AARON MCKINNEY: He wanted a ride home and I just thought, Well, the dude's drunk, let's just take him home.

ROB DEBREE: When did you and Russ talk about jacking him up?

AARON MCKINNEY: We kinda talked about it at the bar.

ROB DEBREE: Okay, what happened next?

AARON MCKINNEY: We drove him out past Wal-Mart. We got over there, and he starts grabbing my leg and grabbing my genitals. I was like, "Look, I'm not a fuckin' faggot. If you touch me again you're gonna get it." I don't know what the hell he was trying to do but I beat him up pretty bad. Think I killed him.

ROB DEBREE: What'd you beat him with?

AARON MCKINNEY: Blacked out. My fist. My pistol. The butt of the gun. Wondering what happened to me. I had a few beers and I don't know. It's like I could see what was going on but I don't know but I don't know, it was like somebody else was doing it.

ROB DEBREE: What was the first thing that he said or that he did in the truck that made you hit him?

AARON MCKINNEY: Well, he put his hand on my leg, slid his hand like as if he was going to grab my balls.

MOMENT: GAY PANIC

ZACKIE SALMON: When that defense team argued that McKinney did what he did because Matthew made a pass at him . . . I just wanted to vomit because that's like saying that it's okay. It's like the "Twinkie Defense," when the guy killed Harvey Milk and Moscone. It's the same thing.

REBECCA HILLIKER: As much as a part of me didn't want the defense of them saying that it was a gay bashing or that it was gay panic, part of me is really grateful. Because I was really scared that in the trial they were going to try and say that it was a robbery, or it was about drugs. So when they used "gay panic" as their defense, I felt this is good, if nothing else the truth is going to be told . . . the truth is coming out.

MOMENT: AARON MCKINNEY (continued)

ROB DEBREE: Did he ever try to defend himself against you or hit you back?

AARON MCKINNEY: Yeah, sort of. He tried his little swings or whatever, but he wasn't very effective.

ROB DEBREE: Okay. How many times did you hit him inside the truck before you guys stopped where you left him?

AARON MCKINNEY: I'd say I hit him two or three times, probably three times with my fists and about six times with the pistol.

ROB DEBREE: Did he ask you to stop?

AARON MCKINNEY: Well, yeah. He was getting the shit kicked out of him.

ROB DEBREE: What did he say?

AARON MCKINNEY: After he asked me to stop most all he was doing was screaming.

ROB DEBREE: So Russ kinda dragged him over to the fence, I'm assuming, and tied him up?

AARON MCKINNEY: Something like that. I just remember Russ was laughing at first but then he got pretty scared.

ROB DEBREE: Was Matthew conscious when Russ tied him up?

AARON MCKINNEY: Yeah. I told him to turn around and don't look at my license plate number 'cause I was scared he would tell the police. And then I asked him what my license plate said. He read it and that's why I hit him a few more times.

ROB DEBREE: Just to be sure? *(Pause)* So obviously you don't like gay people?

AARON MCKINNEY: No, I don't.

ROB DEBREE: Would you say you hate them?

AARON MCKINNEY: Uh, I really don't hate them but, you know, when they start coming on to me and stuff like that I get pretty aggravated.

ROB DEBREE: Did he threaten you?

AARON MCKINNEY: This gay dude?

ROB DEBREE: Yeah.

AARON MCKINNEY: Not really.

ROB DEBREE: Can you answer me one thing? Why'd you guys take his shoes?

AARON MCKINNEY: I don't know. *(Pause)* Now I'm never going to see my son again.

ROB DEBREE: I don't know. You'll probably go to court sometime today.

AARON MCKINNEY: Today? So I'm gonna go in there and just plead guilty or not guilty today?

ROB DEBREE: No, no, you're just going to be arraigned today.

AARON MCKINNEY: He is gonna die for sure?

ROB DEBREE: There is no doubt that Mr. Shepard is going to die.

AARON MCKINNEY: So what are they going to give me, twenty-five to life or just the death penalty and get it over with?

ROB DEBREE: That's not our job. That's the judge's job and the jury.

MOMENT: THE VERDICT

NARRATOR: Has the jury reached a verdict?

FOREPERSON: We have, Your Honor.

We the jury, impaneled and sworn to try the above entitled case, after having well and truly tried the matter, unanimously find as follows:

As to the charge of kidnapping, we find the defendant, Aaron James McKinney, guilty.

As to the charge of aggravated robbery, we find the defendant, Aaron James McKinney, guilty.

As to the charge of first-degree felony murder (kidnapping), we find the defendant, Aaron James McKinney, guilty. *(Verdict goes sotto voce. Narration begins.)*

As to the charge of first-degree felony murder (robbery), we find the defendant, Aaron James McKinney, guilty.

As to the charge of premeditated first-degree murder, we find the defendant, Aaron James McKinney, not guilty.

As to the lesser-included offense of second-degree murder, we find the defendant, Aaron James McKinney, guilty.

MOMENT: DENNIS SHEPARD'S STATEMENT

NARRATOR: Aaron McKinney was found guilty of felony murder which meant the jury could give him the death penalty.
That evening, Judy and Dennis Shepard were approached
by McKinney's defense team, who pled for their client's life.
The following morning, Dennis Shepard made a statement
to the Court. Here is some of what he said.

DENNIS SHEPARD: My son Matthew did not look like a winner.
He was rather uncoordinated and wore braces from the age of
thirteen until the day he died. However, in his all too brief life
he proved that he was a winner. On October sixth, nineteen
ninety-eight, my son tried to show the world that he could
win again. On October twelfth, nineteen ninety-eight, my
firstborn son and my hero, lost. On October twelfth, nineteen
ninety-eight, my firstborn son and my hero died, fifty days
before his twenty-second birthday.

I keep wondering the same thing that I did when I first saw
him in the hospital. What would he have become? How could
he have changed his piece of the world to make it better?

Matt officially died in a hospital in Fort Collins, Colorado. He actually died on the outskirts of Laramie, tied to a
fence. You Mr. McKinney with your friend Mr. Henderson
left him out there by himself, but he wasn't alone. There
were his lifelong friends with him, friends that he had grown
up with. You're probably wondering who these friends were.
First he had the beautiful night sky and the same stars and
moon that we used to see through a telescope. Then he had
the daylight and the sun to shine on him. And through it all
he was breathing in the scent of pine trees from the snowy
range. He heard the wind, the ever-present Wyoming wind,

for the last time. He had one more friend with him, he had God. And I feel better knowing he wasn't alone.

Matt's beating, hospitalization, and funeral focused world-wide attention on hate. Good is coming out of evil. People have said enough is enough. I miss my son, but I am proud to be able to say that he is my son.

Judy has been quoted as being against the death penalty. It has been stated that Matt was against the death penalty. Both of these statements are wrong. Matt believed that there were crimes and incidents that justified the death penalty. I too believe in the death penalty. I would like nothing better than to see you die, Mr. McKinney. However this is the time to begin the healing process. To show mercy to someone who refused to show any mercy. Mr. McKinney, I am going to grant you life, as hard as it is for me to do so, because of Matthew. Every time you celebrate Christmas, a birthday, the Fourth of July remember that Matt isn't. Every time you wake up in your prison cell remember that you had the opportunity and the ability to stop your actions that night. You robbed me of something very precious and I will never forgive you for that. Mr. McKinney I give you life in the memory of one who no longer lives. May you have a long life, and may you thank Matthew every day for it.

MOMENT: AFTERMATH

ROB DEBREE: This is all we've lived and breathed for a year. Daily. This has been my case daily. And now it's over.

OFFICER REGGIE FLUTY: Me and DeBree hugged and cried. . . . And you know, everybody had tears in their eyes, and you're just so thankful you know and Mr. Shepard was cryin' and then that got me bawlin' and everybody just—just kinda like yes: Now we can go on and we can quit being stuck you know?

AARON KREIFELS: It just hit me today, the minute that I got out of the courthouse. That the reason that God wanted me to find him is, for he didn't have to die out there alone, you know. And if I wouldn't of came along, they wouldn't of found him for a couple of weeks at least. So it makes me feel really good that he didn't have to die out there alone.

MATT GALLOWAY: I'm just glad it's over. I really am. Testifying in that trial was one of the hardest things I've ever done. And don't get me wrong, I love the stage, I really do I love it. But it's tricky because basically what you have is lawyers questioning you—from this angle but the answers need to be funneling this way, to the jury. So what you have to do is establish a funneling system. And that's hard for me because I'm a natural conversationalist, so it's just natural instinct that when someone asks you a question, you look at that person to make eye contact. But it's kind of tough when you literally have to scoot over—change your position, in effect, funnel over to where the jury is. But I was able to do that several times over the course of my testimony.

MOMENT: EPILOGUE

ANDY PARIS: On our last trip, I had the good fortune of seeing Jedadiah Schultz play the role of Prior in *Angels in America*. After a performance, we spoke.

JEDADIAH SCHULTZ: I didn't for the longest time let myself become personally involved in the Matthew Shepard thing. It didn't seem real, it just seemed way blown out of proportion. Matthew Shepard was just a name instead of an individual. . . .

I don't know. I just feel bad. Just for all that stuff I told you, for the person I used to be. That's why I want to hear those interviews from last year when I said all that stuff. I don't know. I just can't believe I ever said that stuff about homosexuals, you know. How did I ever let that stuff make me think that you were different from me?

NARRATOR: This is Romaine Patterson.

ROMAINE PATTERSON: Well, a year ago, I wanted to be a rock star. That was my goal. And now, um, well, now it's obviously changed in the fact that, um, throughout the last year I—I've really realized my role in, um, in taking my part. And um, so now instead of going to school to be in music, I'm gonna go to school for communications and political science. Um, because I have a career in political activism.

Actually, I just recently found out I was gonna be honored in Washington, D.C., from the Anti-Defamation League. And whenever I think about the angels or any of the speaking that I've done you know . . . Matthew gave me— Matthew's like guiding this little path with his light for me to walk down. And he just—every time we get to like a door, he opens it. And he just says, "Okay, next step."

And if I get to be a rock star on the side, okay.

NARRATOR: This is Jonas Slonaker.

JONAS SLONAKER: Change is not an easy thing, and I don't think people were up to it here. They got what they wanted. Those two boys got what they deserve, and we look good now. Justice has been served. The OK Corral. We shot down the villains. We sent the prostitutes on the train. The town's cleaned up, and we don't need to talk about it anymore.

You know, it's been a year since Matthew Shepard died, and they haven't passed shit in Wyoming . . . at a state level, any town, nobody anywhere, has passed any kind of laws, antidiscrimination laws or hate crime legislation, nobody has passed anything anywhere. What's come out of it? What's come out of this that's concrete or lasting?

NARRATOR: We all said we would meet again—one last time at the fence.

DOC O'CONNOR: I been up to that site in my limousine, okay? And I remembered to myself the night he and I drove around together, he said to me, "Laramie sparkles, doesn't it?" And where he was up there, if you sit exactly where he was, up there, Laramie sparkles from there, with a low-lying cloud . . . it's the blue lights that's bouncing off the clouds from the airport and it goes *tst tst tst tst* . . . right over the whole city. I mean it blows you away. . . . Matt was right there in that spot, and I can just picture in his eyes, I can just picture what he was seeing. The last thing he saw on this earth was the sparkling lights.

MOMENT: DEPARTURE

MOISÉS KAUFMAN: We've spent the last two days packing a year's worth of materials and saying our good-byes.

LEIGH FONDAKOWSKI: Marge wished us luck, and when we asked her how Laramie would feel seeing a play about itself, she said:

MARGE MURRAY: I think we'd enjoy it. To show it's not the hell-hole of the earth would be nice, but that is up to how you portray us. And that in turn is up to how Laramie behaves.

STEPHEN BELBER: Doc asked me if I wanted to ghostwrite a book about the whole event. Galloway offered me, or anyone else, a place to stay if and when we come back to Laramie. He also seemed interested as to whether there'd be any open auditions for this play.

ANDY PARIS: We left Laramie at about seven in the evening. On the way to Denver, I looked in my rearview mirror to take one last look at the town.

FATHER ROGER SCHMIT: And I will speak with you, I will trust that if you write a play of this, that you say it right. You need to do your best to say it correct.

ANDY PARIS: And in the distance I could see the sparkling lights of Laramie, Wyoming.

END OF PLAY

THE
LARAMIE PROJECT:
TEN YEARS LATER

By Moisés Kaufman,
Leigh Fondakowski,
Greg Pierotti,
Andy Paris,
and Stephen Belber

Dedicated to the memory of Joseph P. Sullivan

THE FACTS

On October 6, 1998, a gay University of Wyoming student, Matthew Shepard, left the Fireside Bar with Aaron McKinney and Russell Henderson. The following day he was discovered at the edge of town. He was tied to a fence, brutally beaten, and close to death.

By the following day, Matthew's attack and the town of Laramie had become the focus of an international news story. On October 12, 1998, Matthew Shepard died at Poudre Valley Hospital in Fort Collins, Colorado.

AUTHORS' NOTE

The Laramie Project had its world premiere at Denver Center Theatre Company in Denver, Colorado, in 2000. At that time, none of us could have imagined the groundswell of interest and productions that would spring up from there. *The Laramie Project* has gone on to be one of the most produced plays in the country for over a decade. As writers we have often been asked—and asked ourselves—why is this so?

One answer is that interest in *The Laramie Project* is a testament to the legacy of Matthew Shepard. His life and his death brought meaning to many lives beyond Laramie.

A second answer comes directly from the participants in the productions themselves. These productions run the spectrum—from professional companies to amateur companies and community theaters to college and high school productions. In the age of social networking and the Internet we often hear directly from these students—their passion for this work is remarkable. We recognize that students, teachers, and administrators have in some cases endeavored to produce *Laramie* at great personal and professional risk; the subjects of hate crime and homophobia have outlined deep divides within some communities.

Laramie is the story of an American town, but it is also the story of ordinary Americans who created a conversation unlike any that had happened up to that point in history. These were ordinary people who faced extraordinary circumstances. Matthew Shepard's murder was a moment in history that revealed both the best and worst in human character and experience.

As a theater company, we had the great privilege of speaking at length with the residents of Laramie, Wyoming, multiple times over the period of a year and a half in the aftermath of the brutal hate crime of Matthew Shepard. Those interviews provided the foundation for the writing of *The Laramie Project*.

Laramie resident Jonas Slonaker asks at the end of *The Laramie Project:* "What's come out of it? What's come out of this that's concrete or lasting?" Ten years later, we decided to return to Laramie to see how the people of the town had changed. We caught up with many of our original interviewees to talk with them again about how their town had changed. We talked to new people as well, including the perpetrators Aaron McKinney and Russell Henderson, as well as Matthew's mother, Judy Shepard.

With the tenth anniversary of Matthew Shepard's murder approaching, Moisés Kaufman, Artistic Director of Tectonic Theater Project, asked, "How does a community write its own history?" Under a microscope for ten years having been associated with such a brutal crime, how has Laramie responded? We have heard people all over the country and all over the world say that Laramie is just like their town. How have we as a nation and as global community responded?

The Laramie Project: Ten Years Later was written as a stand-alone play. That is, it does not have to be performed in conjunction with the original play. However, we hope that the towns and cities and schools across the country who have performed *The Laramie Project* will also perform this epilogue in their communities. And we are excited by the possibility that the two plays could run in repertory to give the full breadth and scope of Laramie's journey.

The world premiere of *The Laramie Project: Ten Years Later* took place on the eleventh anniversary of the death of Matthew Shepard. It was performed at Lincoln Center's Alice Tully Hall by the original cast of *The Laramie Project*. The play was performed simultaneously in more than one hundred and fifty theaters across the country and around the world.

We are honored to be part of this ongoing story of an American town. And we are thrilled to share this conversation with all with you.

On October 12, 2009, Tectonic Theater Project premiered *The Laramie Project: Ten Years Later* simultaneously in one hundred and fifty theaters in all fifty states and eight countries. Presented by each theater with their own casts, the audience was linked with the original cast's performance at Lincoln Center's Alice Tully Hall via live streaming. In this historic theatrical nod to the Federal Theater Project, the play was seen by 50,000 people in one night.

At Alice Tully Hall, the performance was directed by Moisés Kaufman; the scenic consultant was Derek McClane; the lighting design was by Jason Lyons; the dramaturg was Jimmy Maize; and the producers were Greg Reiner and Tiffany Redmon. The cast was as follows:

Kelli Simpkins: Leigh Fondakowski, Zackie Salmon, Jan Lundhurst, Romaine Patterson, Clerk in Wyoming Legislature.

Amanda Gronich: Beth Loffreda, Marge Murray, Girl, *20/20* Narrator.

Greg Pierotti: Himself, Jonas Slonaker, Rob DeBree, University Official, Aaron McKinney.*

Stephen Belber: Himself, Cowboy, Dave O'Malley, Friend #1, George, Republican Man.

Andy Paris: Himself, Matt Michelson, Jedadiah Shultz, Jim Osborne, Jerry Parkinson, Gene Pratt, Boy, Jim, Russell Henderson, Peterson.

Barbara Pitts-McAdams: Catherine Connolly, Grandma, Lucy Thompson, Friend #2, Ben, Judy Shepard.

Mercedes Herrero: Rebecca Hilliker, Reggie Fluty, Deb Thomsen, Susan Swapp, Desk Mate.

John McAdams: Moisés Kaufman, Jeffrey Lockwood, Rental Car Agent, Governor Freudenthal, Dennis Shepard, Father Roger, Glenn Silber, John Dorst, Chairman Childers.

---

* In ensuing productions, the role of Aaron McKinney should not be part of the Greg Pierotti track but part of the Andy Paris track.

CHARACTERS IN ORDER OF APPEARANCE

Narrator

Greg Pierotti—Member, Tectonic Theater Project; early forties.

Beth Loffreda: Professor, University of Wyoming; author of the book *Losing Matt Shepard;* early forties.

Moisés Kaufman—Artistic Director, Tectonic Theater Project; early forties.

Stephen Belber—Member, Tectonic Theater Project; early forties.

Leigh Fondakowski—Member, Tectonic Theater Project; late thirties.

Matt Michelson—Former owner of the Fireside Bar; forties.

Marge Murray— Mother of police officer Reggie Fluty; late sixties.

Jeffrey Lockwood—Laramie resident; fifties.

Jedadiah Shultz—Laramie native; University of Wyoming theater student now living in NYC; early thirties.

Rebecca Hilliker—Theater professor, University of Wyoming; fifties.

Zackie Salmon—Laramie resident, originally from Texas; advocate for domestic partner benefits on campus; fifties.

Andy Paris—Member, Tectonic Theater Project; late thirties.

Cowboy—Laconic man on the street; late forties.

Rental Car Agent—Retired military; early seventies.

Reggie Fluty—Police officer who found Matthew Shepard at the fence; retired; late forties.

Jonas Slonaker—Openly gay Laramie resident; late forties.

Deb Thomsen—Editor of the *Laramie Boomerang*, local Laramie newspaper; early fifties.

Governor Freudenthal—Governor of Wyoming; fifties.

Dave O'Malley—Retired Laramie police officer, lead investigator on the Matthew Shepard case for Laramie Police Department; early fifties.

Catherine Connolly—Out lesbian professor, University of Wyoming; member of the Wyoming legislature; fifties.

Rob DeBree—Lead investigator on the Matthew Shepard case for the Albany County Sheriff's Department; early fifties.

Jim Osborne—Friend of Matthew Shepard; Laramie resident; mid thirties.

Friend #1—Friend of Jim Osborne, early thirties.

Grandma—Grandmother of Friend #1; late seventies.

Mom—A Laramie housewife; early forties.

Dennis Shepard—Father of Matthew Shepard; fifties.

Jerry Parkinson—Dean of the Law School, University of Wyoming; advocate for domestic partner benefits; late forties.

University Official—Late fifties.

Father Roger Schmit—Catholic priest at the Catholic Newman Center in Laramie at the time of Matthew Shepard's murder; sixties.

Lucy Thompson—Grandmother of convicted murderer, Russell Henderson; seventies.

Boy—Current student at University of Wyoming; late teens.

Girl—Current student at University of Wyoming, late teens.

Jan Lundhurst—Laramie resident; late forties.

20/20 Narrator—Newscaster; late thirties.

Glenn Silber—Producer, *20/20;* early fifties.

Romaine Patterson—Friend of Matthew Shepard; gay activist; early thirties.

Boomerang Editor—Played by actor who plays Deb Thomsen, early fifties.

Friend #2—Friend of Jim Osborne; early twenties.

John Dorst—Professor, University of Wyoming; folklorist and Laramie resident; mid fifties.

George—Laramie resident; guest at potluck dinner party; fifties.

Ben—Laramie resident; guest at potluck dinner party; forties.

Jim—Laramie resident; guest at potluck dinner party; forties.

Susan Swapp—University of Wyoming professor and Laramie resident; mid fifties.

Russell Henderson—Convicted murderer of Matthew Shepard; early thirties.

Clerk—Chief clerk in Wyoming legislature; mid thirties.

Peterson—Republican Representative in Wyoming legislature; late sixties.

Desk Mate—Catherine Connolly's desk mate in the legislature; early forties.

Conservative Colleague—Catherine Connolly's colleague in the legislature; early fifties.

Childers—Conservative Representative in Wyoming legislature; early seventies.

Republican Man—Catherine Connolly's colleague in Wyoming legislature; early fifties.

Aaron McKinney—Convicted murderer of Matthew Shepard; early thirties.

Judy Shepard—Mother of Matthew Shepard; fifties.

ACT I

(The sound of wind. The sound of many voices speaking. At first in whispers, then a little louder. Lights come up onstage. The space is littered with chairs. All facing the audience. They suggest the homes and the characters that inhabit Laramie. BETH LOFFREDA enters. She's wearing a coat or a vest to protect her from the cold. She looks around remembering.)

MOMENT: THE LIGHT THIS FALL

BETH LOFFREDA: I am thinking about the anniversary a lot. Ten years have passed . . . that's a long time. *(Pause)* The light this fall is much like the light that fall and we've been having days that remind me of that fall when Matt was killed . . . so there's something about the elemental reality here that feels intensely like that September and October when all of this happened. That was nineteen ninety-eight. *(Pause. Pointing out her window)* You can see the prairie and the foothills from some offices on campus. You can look out the window and you can see a little patch of the foothills, you know, past Wal-Mart, where Matthew died.

So what happened here still feels very present to me.

My gut reaction is that Laramie is a somewhat better place to be than it was ten years ago, but I don't know how to tell the story of the past ten years without having to think about, both what we've done, but also what we haven't done.

(Transition. The company enters.)

MOMENT: GOOD ENERGY

MOISÉS KAUFMAN: September twelfth. On our way to Laramie again.

NARRATOR: Company member Moisés Kaufman.

MOISÉS KAUFMAN: The anniversary of Matthew's death is exactly one month away. Arriving into town off Highway 80, I am surprised by how much the town has grown.

LEIGH FONDAKOWSKI: There is an explosion of new development on the east side.

NARRATOR: Company member Leigh Fondakowski.

LEIGH FONDAKOWSKI: At least three brand new hotels and several strip malls. Wal-Mart has been replaced by Super Wal-Mart.

MATT MICKELSON: How has Laramie changed?

NARRATOR: Matt Mickelson, former owner of the Fireside Bar.

MATT MICKELSON: These days in Wyoming with the coal-bed methane boom and—the energy industry—like Dick Cheney sold half our state to Halliburton. But people don't seem to mind.

MARGE MURRAY: Yeah, they're drillin' all over now.

NARRATOR: Marge Murray.

MARGE MURRAY: They are and they should. And we have so much coal that it's unreal. No matter where you go, you poke a hole in the ground and you'll find some coal. And it's good energy.

JEFFREY LOCKWOOD: The position Wyoming is in right now economically, there's plenty of money.

NARRATOR: Laramie resident Jeffrey Lockwood.

JEFFREY LOCKWOOD: The recession hasn't touched us here. We've been having a big energy boom and they're talking about it being a thirty-year boom.

JEDADIAH SCHULTZ: The entire shape of Laramie has changed.

NARRATOR: Laramie native Jedadiah Schultz.

JEDADIAH SCHULTZ: We have a Chili's now. Laramie has a lot more of those kinds of—like little modern mini-mall things. The university is booming with money so they just build, build, build and they've got a huge Hilton and a Holiday Inn and a convention center.

JEFFREY LOCKWOOD: Now, some of these communities that they're drilling in are just getting hammered in terms of the environment—the goose that's laying the golden egg is crapping all over you but it's still producing golden eggs.

REBECCA HILLIKER: On the surface things have changed here.

NARRATOR: Rebecca Hilliker, theater department, University of Wyoming.

REBECCA HILLIKER: Just look around you at the physical growth. But whether or not we have changed the underlying culture of Wyoming at all, I don't know.

JIM OSBORNE: After the media storm died down here in Laramie—

NARRATOR: Jim Osborne, friend of Matthew Shepard.

JIM OSBORNE: There were a lot of folks who simply didn't want to talk about Matthew Shepard anymore. They were tired of their community and their lives being the nightly news. They were tired of feeling the stigma of having such a heinous crime occur in our community.

JOHN DORST: This was all anyone talked about in terms of what Laramie is and Wyoming is.

NARRATOR: Laramie resident John Dorst.

JOHN DORST: There was I think a palpable sense here in Laramie of just, "Let's stop talking about this, please, let's return to business as usual."

MOMENT: REGGIE AND MARGE

NARRATOR: Company member Greg Pierotti.

GREG PIEROTTI: I drive out to meet with Reggie Fluty, the officer who found Matthew Shepard at the fence.

REGGIE FLUTY: Well, I am no longer working on the force now.

GREG PIEROTTI: Really?

REGGIE FLUTY: Yep. I'm retired.

MARGE MURRAY: Her horses are her work now.

GREG PIEROTTI: We also speak with her mom, Marge Murray.

MARGE MURRAY: Ask her what she named her horses—

GREG PIEROTTI: What'd you name your horses?

REGGIE FLUTY: Boogeyman, Reno, and Mad Marge.

MARGE MURRAY: She named a horse after me.

REGGIE FLUTY: I told her, "I am riding a horse that reminds me of you on a bad day."

MARGE MURRAY: *(Smiling)* The brat. . . . And she still has her llamas—

REGGIE FLUTY: And we have a couple of new colts.

MARGE MURRAY: But you asked us how our lives have changed? Biggest change would be Reggie's not working on the force now.

REGGIE FLUTY: After I retired, I had to learn how to sleep again and how to be a normal citizen again. Not live in code yellow like everywhere you go somebody's ready to sucker punch you, you know?

MARGE MURRAY: After Shepard, it was hell for her. And after the main crisis was over, every time there was a high profile case, like girls getting raped or babies dying—they only knew one phone number: Reggie's. So it finally got to her.

REGGIE FLUTY: I did those kinds of cases for so long that I got exhausted. Those can burn you out pretty fast. Now the horses, they don't give a damn if I am a police officer or an ordinary citizen. You know, with them, it's all about "when's feedin' time?"
    But as far as Laramie is concerned, I do think people's views have changed. I think we were so embarrassed the first time that we don't want that to happen again. And sometimes you know, you gotta just as a community get the snot slugged out of you before you wake up and grow up, you know?

MARGE MURRAY: Well, there were two things, though, that I really hated. Tearing that fence down and not puttin' up some kind of . . . something to say "This is where it happened. Straighten up, Laramie."

GREG PIEROTTI: They took the fence down?

MARGE MURRAY: Yeah, they did.

REGGIE FLUTY: The owner didn't want people coming out onto his property to see it—there's "no trespassing" signs all over there now.

GREG PIEROTTI: Wow.

REGGIE FLUTY: I just hope the community remembers truly how ugly hate is. Every time there's an anniversary of his death, talk comes back up. And it makes people have to own what they think. If you hang around Laramie long enough, you'll know where everybody stands.

MOMENT: SECOND AND GARFIELD (COWBOY)

NARRATOR: Company member Andy Paris.

ANDY PARIS: One of the first things we do when we get to Laramie this time is walk around the town conducting informal interviews. Moisés and I are waiting out a storm under the awning of the Laramie Health Clinic on Second and Garfield. A cowboy steps out of the clinic for a smoke.

ANDY PARIS: Good afternoon.

COWBOY: How ya doin'.

ANDY PARIS: Just waitin' out the rain under here.

MOISÉS KAUFMAN: We're here from New York with a theater company.
(Pause. COWBOY *doesn't answer.)*

We're here finding out how Laramie has changed since the Matthew Shepard murder.
(Pause. COWBOY doesn't answer.)

Can we ask you a couple of questions?
(Pause)

COWBOY: No.
(COWBOY goes back inside.)

ANDY PARIS: That went well.

MOMENT: THIRD AND CUSTER

RENTAL CAR AGENT: Mid-sized car okay for you, Mr. Belber?

STEPHEN BELBER: That'll be just fine.

RENTAL CAR AGENT: You're here for the big game?

STEPHEN BELBER: Actually, I'm here with a theater company, we are writing a play about the town ten years after the death of Matthew Shepard.

RENTAL CAR AGENT: Well, I wish you luck with your project, but I do think it's time to let the boy go. Now if you ask me, I think it was robbery and that his lifestyle was just an excuse. His lifestyle's beside the point. It makes no difference to me.

STEPHEN BELBER: Do you think it made a difference to his killers?

RENTAL CAR AGENT: No, I don't. No. I think they set out to rob him, found out about his lifestyle, and then in the trial used it as an excuse. . . .

STEPHEN BELBER: *(Surprised)* I'm not sure I understand. Are you saying that it wasn't a hate crime?

RENTAL CAR AGENT: Well, I just think people have agendas and they keep coming here pushing their agendas and they're keeping that boy stuck. I think it's time to let the boy go. I think it's time to let go and let the young man get on with his life—or with his death—course, I believe in an afterlife.

Excuse me but I have to attend to this gentleman. You enjoy your stay in Laramie.

STEPHEN BELBER: Thank you.

MOMENT: *BOOMERANG* #1—DEB THOMSEN

MOISÉS KAUFMAN: With the anniversary of Matthew's death approaching, I call Deb Thomsen, the editor of the main paper here in Laramie.

DEB THOMSEN: *Laramie Boomerang.*

MOISÉS KAUFMAN: Hi, may I please speak with Deb?

DEB THOMSEN: Speaking.

MOISÉS KAUFMAN: Deb, this is Moisés Kaufman, how are you?

DEB THOMSEN: *(Pause) (Hesitates)* Hi, I'm fine, thanks.

MOISÉS KAUFMAN: Good. So do you have a moment to talk?

DEB THOMSEN: No problem.

MOISÉS KAUFMAN: So tell me, as editor of the main paper here in Laramie, how have the people been thinking about the anniversary?

DEB THOMSEN: Actually, we're doing a short series. I'm doing the intro piece and one of the other reporters has been talking with people just to get their perspective now.

MOISÉS KAUFMAN: And besides the series, what kinds of events are planned for the anniversary of Matthew's murder?

DEB THOMSEN: Well . . . events . . . here in Laramie? That would be more something that is organized on campus. But to be quite honest with you, we're long past this. . . . You know, we're trying to put this behind us, and keep going. You have brutality and you deal with it, and you move on.

MOISÉS KAUFMAN: Mm hmm?

DEB THOMSEN: I do think that it brought forth a different awareness. . . . I hesitate to speak on behalf of the community, but I don't believe that the catalyst was homosexuality.

MOISÉS KAUFMAN: What do you mean?

DEB THOMSEN: I really believe they wanted money. And Matthew didn't have what they thought and it just escalated to an anger that was totally out of control. There was so much speculation about drug use. I just don't think it was about his sexuality.

MOISÉS KAUFMAN: *(Surprised)* So you don't think it was a hate crime?

DEB THOMSEN: I think everything is a hate crime. You have to have some kind of hatred in you to do that to another human being. As far as where that hatred comes from, I really couldn't tell you. Most people in the community, they're aware of what's happened here, they know that the anniversary is coming up, but we really are moving on from this.

MOMENT: MEASURING CHANGE #1

NARRATOR: Leigh Fondakowski.

LEIGH FONDAKOWSKI: I drive up to Cheyenne, the state capitol, to speak with Wyoming Governor Dave Freudenthal.
   (To GOVERNOR*)* Governor, one of the things we are hearing in Laramie is some people now saying that this was not a hate crime.

GOVERNOR FREUDENTHAL: I haven't heard that. *(Beat)* I don't know where you are hearing that. It may be that there are people who want to dismiss it. I don't share that view. It happened here. And we have to own that. When people think about Matthew Shepard's murder, it's not a particularly proud moment in the state's history or the community's history.
   And I would say that there has been a change in general in the state with regard to more thoughtful discussion. If you just say the words "Matthew Shepard" it registers with people. At least people in my generation. I can tell you that it has a different feel about how we talk about things.

How do you *measure* change is the thing I'm stuck with.

I mean, the events surrounding the death of Matthew Shepard changed us—it clearly did. How you measure that change, I'm not quite sure.

DAVE O'MALLEY: *(Answering the* GOVERNOR, *enthusiastically)* Well, I tell you what, we now have the AIDS Walk here in Laramie, it's in its sixth year, okay?

NARRATOR: Dave O'Malley, retired Laramie police officer.

DAVE O'MALLEY: And it's grown. Last year we raised around twenty-two thousand dollars. And five thousand dollars at drag queen bingo alone! I mean we had the drag queens at the Cowboy Bar, Jim and Jason and Travis, and they put on just a great production you know. Yeah, at the *Cowboy* Bar!

CATHERINE CONNOLLY: On campus the biggest difference would be the symposium for social justice.

NARRATOR: Catherine Connolly, university professor.

CATHERINE CONNOLLY: The name changed to the *Shepard* Symposium for Social Justice several years ago, and not only is it a university conference but kids from all over Wyoming are coming to the Shepard Symposium. Great big yellow school buses of kids coming in to hear these speakers talk about justice and social change. And you get thousands of people from the town participating, and for this town, that's a lot of people. So, I'm giving you the good.

JIM OSBORNE: Before Matt's murder, nobody talked much about gay and lesbian people or issues in Wyoming.

NARRATOR: Jim Osborne, friend of Matthew Shepard.

JIM OSBORNE: Now, there's a Rainbow Resource center on campus, we have more gender and sexuality classes, the high school has a gay-straight alliance. I am openly gay. And I've heard from a lot of folks in Laramie over the years who say to me things like:

FRIEND #1: Jim, my grandmother watched a news story and she called me and she said:

GRANDMA: You know what, honey I just wanted you to know it doesn't matter to me if you're gay.

FRIEND #1: But Grandma, I'm straight.

GRANDMA: Well, but if you were.

FRIEND #1: Well, thank you Grandma.

JIM OSBORNE: Or folks who come to me and say:

MOM: My husband makes . . . comments. What if my five-year-old son happens to grow up to be gay? I don't want him to be afraid his father's going to hate him. How can I let my kids know that it's okay with me, you know?

JIM OSBORNE: So we don't have a hate crimes law on the books, but the conversations that go on in our locker rooms, in the hallways at schools, on the playgrounds, in our living rooms, and places of worship. That to me is progress.

MOMENT: SAFE POCKET

JONAS SLONAKER: For me the biggest change from then to now is that I am completely out now.

NARRATOR: Jonas Slonaker.

JONAS SLONAKER: After Matt was killed I was gonna leave Laramie. But I went to the vigil for Matthew Shepard and I met Bill there. . . . *(Smile)* We started seeing each other . . . and we have been together ever since—ten years. Everybody knows that Bill is my boyfriend, but I am in a safe pocket and the safe pocket is the university. I'm in student affairs and that's a really safe place to be. Now if I were in Ag? Agriculture? It would be different. Or you know if I worked at the cement factory here in Laramie, it's a different world. But I mean, finding your safe pockets is what we do as gay people not just here in Laramie but wherever we live.

MOMENT: BENCH DEDICATION

ANDY PARIS: With the anniversary of Matthew's death now only two weeks away we spoke to Beth Loffreda about what the university is doing to mark the day.

BETH LOFFREDA: The university held a ceremony dedicating a memorial bench in the name of Matthew Shepard. The bench is tucked away in a remote corner of the campus. It was a small ceremony. There were only about fifty people there. It was a Saturday morning. It was chilly and then, in that way that happens here in Laramie as if a switch has been flipped, all at once blazingly warm. There was a podium beside the bench. Dennis Shepard spoke. When he got up to speak, you could see that his nose was scratched and bruised.

DENNIS SHEPARD: *(Soberly)* Good morning. Judy and I both attended University of Wyoming and we loved it. It's nice to be back on campus again. As you can see, I had a little accident. I broke my nose doing work around the house. My son Matt and I had a competition when he was alive. We each had broken our noses twice, one of us would pull ahead of the other for a while and then the other would tie it back up again. And Matt would make fun of me for being behind. *(Pause)* When Matt was lying in the hospital, unconscious, one of his many injuries was a broken nose. It was Matt's third, one more than me. Now I have restored the tie. *(Beat)* This is a place for people to come. If they are aware of who Matt was. This is a place where they can come and sit and think. A lot of people come to Laramie and they want go out and find the fence. Well, the fence is no longer there. So what they can do instead is they can come here. *(Beat)* Matt was just a normal—a normal kid who had dreams and ambitions. He wanted to work overseas—to promote the country that he loved. He wasn't ashamed of who he was. Or, who he loved. *(Beat)* We want to thank you all for attending this morning. We hope people enjoy the bench.

ZACKIE SALMON: Matthew's legacy—his main legacy is right here at the University of Wyoming.

NARRATOR: Zackie Salmon.

ZACKIE SALMON: And I just felt there was a certain forgetfulness in the air that morning the bench was dedicated . . . because we've worked, worked, worked, worked, worked to get domestic partner benefits here on campus, and we still don't have that.

BETH LOFREDDA: If there was gonna be a place that I would have expected change to happen more quickly . . . it would be right here at the University of Wyoming.

ZACKIE SALMON: Those of us who have been fighting for this, we call ourselves the "gang of four"—and that's Beth Loffreda, myself, Cathy Connolly, and Jerry Parkinson, dean of the law school.

JERRY PARKINSON: We were all optimistic after last year with the Domestic Partner Initiative. We brought in a consultant to tell us how to get domestic partner benefits and we came up with a plan.

CATHERINE CONNOLLY: And at the start of the semester, we thought we were gonna have this implemented.

JERRY PARKINSON: But just when it's about to come to a vote, they tell us:

UNIVERSITY OFFICIAL: There's gonna be a couple of trustees who are totally opposed to this on moral grounds, and we don't agree with their views but . . . give us some time to talk to those folks and talk about the business necessity.

JERRY PARKINSON: *(To* UNIVERSITY OFFICIAL*)* Look, sooner or later you just have to take a vote and the two or three trustees who are gonna vote against it are gonna show their true colors.

UNIVERSITY OFFICIAL: Okay. We don't want them saying things about domestic partner benefits in the press that could hurt the cause. We don't know what they'll do.

JERRY PARKINSON: *(To* UNIVERSITY OFFICIAL*)* They're the ones who look bad in this deal. It's not the people proposing the domestic partner benefits that look bad.

ZACKIE SALMON: What about people like me? I have been with my partner Anne for twenty years and she doesn't get any of my benefits. You don't seem too worried about upsetting me?

UNIVERSITY OFFICIAL: We have all the sympathy in the world, Zackie, and we understand, but look, we don't want to run the risk if we push this too precipitously.

ZACKIE SALMON: It's been ten years that we've been fighting. This is not the nineteen-fifties anymore. It's time for Laramie to come into the twenty-first century. A bench to Matthew Shepard is nice—but a university's values are reflected in its policies.

JERRY PARKINSON: There are so many people out there around the country who don't know anything about Laramie. But they really believe in their hearts that the University of Wyoming would be the last place in the country to adopt same sex partner benefits. And at the rate we're goin' . . . we *are* gonna be the last.

BETH LOFFREDA: A lot of us who work here at the university and a lot of administrators can look out our windows and can see the place where Matthew Shepard died, where he was slaughtered; I just think if that's not enough to get you off the blocks to *really* make some active significant changes on your campus . . . I don't know what it takes.

DENNIS SHEPARD: There is a plaque here which reads, "Matthew Wayne Shepard December first, nineteen-seventy-six, to October twelfth, nineteen ninety-eight. Beloved son, brother, and friend. He continues to make a difference. Peace be with him and all who sit here." Thank you very much.

MOMENT: NEXT GENERATION

(Acting note: These students should not be played dumb or for laughs. They should be played as regular college kids who have not been given information about this one issue.)

NARRATOR: Greg Pierotti.

GREG PIEROTTI: I walk around campus to see if I can meet some students—to talk with the next generation about how they see things now. . . .

    I see a young couple getting into their car. Excuse me, can I ask you: Did you happen to attend the bench dedication for Matthew Shepard?

BOY: Excuse me.

GIRL: For who?

GREG PIEROTTI: For Matthew Shepard. *(Pause)* Do you remember him or what happened to him?

BOY: I don't know anything about him.

GREG PIEROTTI: You never heard anything?

BOY: I heard the name, that's about it.

GREG PIEROTTI: How about you?

GIRL: I heard he was homosexual and he got murdered. He got put somewhere like on a post somewhere *(she points vaguely toward the campus)* and he got murdered.

GREG PIEROTTI: And how long have you been at the university?

GIRL: Two years.

GREG PIEROTTI: How about you?

BOY: Yeah, two years.
(Another STUDENT walks by.)

GREG PIEROTTI: I talked to a number of other students about what they remembered:

STUDENT: One thing I heard was that he was a drug dealer and did some bad deals and those guys ended up coming after him.

GREG PIEROTTI: So you don't think this murder was about Matthew being gay?

STUDENT: I'm not saying that's right. I am just telling you what I heard.

GREG PIEROTTI: Okay.

STUDENT: And then the media came in and said it was 'cause he was gay for their own ends. They took this as a vehicle.

GREG PIEROTTI: And you heard this from?

STUDENT: It seems like there are a lot of students sayin' it so I figured they knew what they were talking about.

MOMENT: *20/20*

NARRATOR: Cathy Connolly.

CATHERINE CONNOLLY: There was a generation or two generations of students who came to this university believing that the story of Matthew Shepard was relevant. That this was part of their history and they wanted to know more about it. And they were aware that they were in the same rooms, walking the same little paths that both Matthew and the perpetrators walked. But now, new students don't come to the university either knowing or caring or thinking it's relevant to their lives. . . .

Because here is what else is going on with Matthew Shepard.

There was a *20/20* episode that came out in two thousand and four—six years after Matthew was killed—and the implication of that TV program was that it wasn't a hate crime, but a robbery or drug deal gone bad. And people here in Laramie at that time were pretty livid given the inaccuracies.

DAVE O'MALLEY: When *20/20* called me for an interview . . .

NARRATOR: Dave O'Malley, lead investigator on the Shepard case for the Laramie Police Department.

DAVE O'MALLEY: I asked them "What exactly are you all doing?" And they said:

GLENN SILBER: It's an objective, what's-going-on-six-years-after type of a thing.

DAVE O'MALLEY: They came to our house and the producer Glenn Silber and Elizabeth Vargas, and my wife, Jen, and I sat at *that* table *(he points to his living room table)*. And I asked them, "Is there any specific focus that you are directing this piece to?"

GLENN SILBER: "No no no no, don't worry about that."

DAVE O'MALLEY: And Elizabeth Vargas went in our bathroom and changed clothes and we set up and did the interview. And shortly into it, it popped straight to the methamphetamine thing.

20/20 NARRATOR: November twenty-sixth, two thousand and four—Good evening and welcome to *20/20*.

  The killing of Matthew Shepard was widely perceived as a hate crime, because Matthew was gay, but over the next hour, you will hear a very different account from the killers themselves and from new sources that have come forward for the first time. A *20/20* investigation uncovers stunning new information about one of this country's most infamous murders.

  You may think you know what happened next, but you haven't heard the whole story.

JAN LUNDHURST: It was very shocking to me to see that.

NARRATOR: Laramie resident Jan Lundhurst.

JAN LUNDHURST: They were interviewing the murderers after they'd been in prison for many years, and I thought, well, yeah, you can change your story however you want to now. They completely changed what they had said in their confessions.

DAVE O'MALLEY: It angered me more than anything the things *20/20 didn't* say—the things they left out. I mean how do you come in and a) lie to me but b) put a piece together that's based solely on meth heads from the Buckhorn Bar and two convicted murderers. And I'm just goin' "holy crap!" *(Holding up the email)* After they left I found a hard copy of an e-mail from Glenn Silber to Elizabeth Vargas, and I can give you a copy of it, it said:

GLENN SILBER: Although Dave is a highly skilled investigator and was the key to solving the crime quickly, he fell into the hate crimes motivation early and our piece will ultimately discredit that flawed theory.

DAVE O'MALLEY: And I read that and I went these assho—excuse me . . . I . . . get a little angry. These guys sit in my house . . . and lie to me. And Silber drives all the way back to Colorado and our phone rings and he says:

GLENN SILBER: Uhh. . . . Did we leave anything there?

DAVE O'MALLEY: And I said, "Yeah and my wife has already scanned it and sent it to Judy Shepard, and she sent it to her attorney in D.C. and you can come back and get it if you want to." And he drove all the way back from Denver and—I-I-I'm not a violent individual but I really did want to choke him. *(Beat)* And we used to watch *20/20* every week. . . .

JIM OSBORNE: Some folks here in Laramie want to find any excuse as to why this happened.

NARRATOR: Jim Osborne, friend of Matthew Shepard.

JIM OSBORNE: They want to write this murder off. And a big part of how people do that is *20/20*.

You had a major, respected news source who came up with this set of stories that said, "Okay, it wasn't really about the fact that he was gay, it was really about *this*."

DAVE O'MALLEY: PBS did a nice rebuttal, they went point by point through the entire thing pointing out the false statements, the leading questions, the quotes taken out of context . . . but how many people watch PBS and how many people watch *20/20*?

CATHERINE CONNOLLY: *(Frustrated)* There were facts revealed in the trial, the reality of the actual confession, everything that happened in the trial gave us the truth . . . and we thought because it was the truth and the truth played out here—that the truth would prevail. But the reality is, that over time, that *20/20* piece has made a tremendous negative impact on how Matthew Shepard's murder is perceived. And this is—this is personal—there's a perception and belief now that it was a drug deal gone bad and that's all. So you asked me how I felt? I go catatonic after things like this. This is our history.

MOMENT: FATHER ROGER

NARRATOR: Greg Pierotti.

GREG PIEROTTI: Today I spoke to Father Roger, the Catholic priest who hosted the vigil for Matthew in Laramie ten years ago, and who also visited with Aaron McKinney in jail, counseled him. Father Roger is no longer in Laramie. I spoke to him by phone.

FATHER ROGER: I left Laramie in two thousand and two. I took a sabbatical and then I was placed in Kansas City.

GREG PIEROTTI: And where did you go on sabbatical?

FATHER ROGER: To Menlo Park, the Vatican II institute. A great place. If you ever get ordained as a Catholic priest, Greg, go there for your sabbatical.

GREG PIEROTTI: *(Beat)* Father, I just completely lost my train of thought. *(Beat)* Oh yeah, how have you been changed personally by this?

FATHER ROGER: I'm much more courageous now than I was before Matthew. I talk about sexual identity a lot more. I don't talk about it every Sunday, but I do talk about it whenever the scriptures enable it to happen.

GREG PIEROTTI: Do you miss Laramie, Father?

FATHER ROGER: Oh my, yes, I miss Laramie. I will always miss Laramie.

GREG PIEROTTI: And are you still in touch with Aaron McKinney?

FATHER ROGER: Yes, I have visited with Aaron often, went to see him a bunch of times. Aaron was in Rawlins, Wyoming, for a couple of years, and now he is in Virginia, and we still write.

GREG PIEROTTI: Do you think we should try to interview him?

FATHER ROGER: Should you try? I hope you do. And let me tell you why. Aaron McKinney and Russell Henderson are products of our society. They are our brothers also. I don't say this in any way at all to excuse him; if you hear that, you are misunderstanding me. But to understand does not mean to agree with. To understand does not mean to be permissive. But to understand also isn't the kind of thing that you decide in your office. To understand Aaron, you have to visit him.

GREG PIEROTTI: I'll send Aaron a letter today asking if he would be willing to meet with me.

FATHER ROGER: Yes Greg, I think you *must* do that. I think you must. *(Beat)* Let me give you an analogy. Several years ago a man came into our monastery and shot four of our monks, and then went into our church and shot himself. When the investigators came to take the bodies away, one of them asked Abbot Gregory, "Well, listen, we'll bring a separate vehicle to take the body of the person who killed them." And Gregory said, "No, he too is our brother. You can put them all in the same ambulance." Now you go back to this. Matthew is our brother; Russell is our brother; Aaron is our brother. And Greg, Aaron is much more like me than unlike me.

MOMENT: LUCY THOMPSON

STEPHEN BELBER: As Greg was talking to Father Roger, I was trying to find a way to talk to Russell Henderson. And so I met again with Gene Pratt, who was Russell Henderson's Mormon home teacher. After the murders, Russell was excommunicated from the Mormon Church. But Mr. Pratt remained close to the family. This time around he did something he hadn't been willing to do ten years earlier. He set up a meeting with Lucy Thompson, Russell's grandmother.

LEIGH FONDAKOWSKI: She was much older and frailer than the woman we'd seen read a statement at Russell's sentencing ten years earlier.

STEPHEN BELBER: On her wall there were pencil sketchings of Jesus—finely drawn, exquisitely detailed.

LUCY THOMPSON: Russell did those drawings in jail and sent them to me. Aren't they something? I tried to mail him some pencils and some sketchbooks. But he can't have art supplies where he's at now in Virginia. When he was in Rawlins he could. He got his GED in Rawlins too and he went to take college classes, chose his courses, got his books sent and was all excited, and then they said, "All right, it's time for you to be transferred." That happened to him twice. So he never did get to do that—go to college.

STEPHEN BELBER: Mrs. Thompson, we would very much like to interview Russell. Do you think he would talk to us?

LUCY THOMPSON: *(Pause)* I don't know. You can try writing to him. And I'll tell him that we talked today, he calls me pretty regularly. But it will be up to him.

STEPHEN BELBER: Thank you.

MOMENT: *BOOMERANG* #2—"OUR VIEW"

NARRATOR: Andy Paris.

ANDY PARIS: Over the course of our stay in Laramie, there had been a couple of articles printed in the *Laramie Boomerang* about Matthew Shepard. These were the articles that the editor Deb Thomsen had mentioned to Moisés. This morning, on October twelfth, the tenth anniversary of Matthew's death, I got a call from Jonas Slonaker. And he said:

JONAS SLONAKER: Did you see the *Laramie Boomerang* this morning? You've got to read the editorial. You're not going to believe it, it's called:

BOOMERANG EDITOR: "Our View. Laramie is a community not a 'project.'"

The recent news story in the *Boomerang* looking back to the brutal murder of Matthew Shepard ten years ago has drawn a wide range of reactions from this community. The biggest reaction has come from those who don't understand why this anniversary qualifies as news.

Some callers have requested that their paper delivery be held during the week that the series of stories was being published. Others have accepted that the local newspaper had to do a story about the anniversary given the national notoriety but wished that the coverage could have been less detailed and displayed more discreetly.

JONAS SLONAKER: Can you believe that?

BOOMERANG EDITOR: A far smaller number of messages have come from people who wanted much more exhaustive reporting.

Direct observation and discussion with the wide range of local residents tells us that Laramie is like most communities but more tolerant than most. That doesn't mean there aren't prejudiced or bigoted people here. There are. But those people don't define Laramie, and it is infuriating for those of us who consider this our home to be labeled because of the actions of a few questionable characters.

That label is particularly galling in this case because the crime in question has been portrayed in the national media as a homophobic attack and as a hate crime because Matthew Shepard was homosexual. But no one can know that motivation except for the two men who committed the crime.

JONAS SLONAKER: Andy, they had a trial and it was established as a hate crime. That's why they had a trial. That's what a trial is for, so that we can learn these things!

BOOMERANG EDITOR: Police records certainly seem to indicate that this was a robbery that went very bad.

JONAS SLONAKER: What police records are they referring to? A robbery? I tie you up and smash your head in because I want to rob you? It's absurd! And this is Laramie's main newspaper.

BOOMERANG EDITOR: But those who wanted to label Laramie as a bigoted town in the Wild West didn't let the facts get in the way of their stories. So who then is guilty of intolerance and perpetuating stereotypes?

JONAS SLONAKER: *(Angry)* A robbery gone bad over drugs, that's denial. That's some kind of massive denial.

ANDY PARIS: Jonas wrote a letter to the editor.

JONAS SLONAKER: Many citizens of Laramie want to move on but denial isn't the best way to accomplish that. There is no disgrace for Laramie in acknowledging that part or all of the motivation in the murder of Matthew Shepard was homophobia. NO, the crime certainly does not define Laramie. How we react to the crime, how we talk about it, and if we do or don't do anything to prevent this from happening again does define Laramie.

ANDY PARIS: Then he told me:

JONAS SLONAKER: Andy, I can't wait to hear what people say when my letter goes to print.

MOMENT: VISIBLE MARKERS

NARRATOR: Stephen Belber.

STEPHEN BELBER: I spend the afternoon with Matt Mickelson, former owner of the Fireside Bar. The fence has been taken down. The Fireside where Matthew met his killers has been renamed JJ's. It seems like all the visible markers of Matthew's death are gone.

MATT MICKELSON: Yeah, I had to sell the Fireside. On one side people were like, "Local Gay Bar!" and then on the other they're like, "Crazy Redneck Gay Slayers!" For seven years—I tried to ride that shit out. Then, MTV'd make a movie, so I'd renovate and paint and do all this shit. Then HBO'd make a movie. NBC'd make a movie. *20/20*'d make a movie. They drug that shit out for seven fuckin' years—so, instead of havin' kids crawlin' in the windows on a Friday night, it was a ghost town. Man, I did eight hundred and some thousand dollars in sales that year that Matt was killed. The next year I did forty-three thousand, crushed me. I had put that shit up for sale.

STEPHEN BELBER: And then I asked Mickelson about the *Boomerang* editorial:

MATT MICKELSON: I tried to tell people—it was such a big media sensationalism hate crime hate crime hate crime—it's not—that wasn't the issue. The issue was methamphetamines. They'd been up for three days, those two guys had been up for three days doin' dope. And that's why they beat him and robbed him.

NARRATOR: Jim Osborne.

JIM OSBORNE: One of my friends a couple months back said to me:

FRIEND #2: I know what really happened, I've talked with people, I know what really happened. It was drugs.

JIM OSBORNE: And I looked at her and I said, "You were eight when Matt was killed. How in the hell do you know what really happened? You were eight and not living in this town. But somehow you know?"

REGGIE FLUTY: Yeah, I've heard about people who say it wasn't a hate crime.

NARRATOR: Reggie Fluty.

REGGIE FLUTY: Nobody says that to me. And if they do, it gets shut down so fast. I won't discuss it. It's not an option, it's bullshit and I'm not wasting my time or theirs.

MOMENT: *BOOMERANG* #3—THE STORY WE'VE TOLD OURSELVES

JONAS SLONAKER: I waited all week for the *Laramie Boomerang* to print my letter. And it finally got to the next Sunday and it never appeared. And there was a letter from a guy lamenting the fact that not enough people are coming to the football games and I was like, "Well jeez, there's plenty of room for my letter *(fighting tears)* they just didn't do it." And I said to my partner Bill, "We're in this little world where everything's okay like in our neighborhood and in our jobs, but there's all these people around us that are thinkin' this shit." And, I drove out to the prairie and screamed until my throat hurt. It really broke my spirit when they refused to print my letter. What am I gonna do with this? You know, what AM I gonna do?

JEFFREY LOCKWOOD: Laramie had this moment. There was a moment of self-reflection.

NARRATOR: Jeffrey Lockwood.

JEFFREY LOCKWOOD: But it was just too frightening. The Matthew Shepard murder flies in the face of who we are, the story we've told ourselves and so you've either got to radically adjust your story or you've got to throw out the data. And so far what we've done is throw out the data.

REGGIE FLUTY: Shame is a funny thing. It makes you really look at yourself hard, you know? And when you have that kind of thing happen in your town, and it hurts a whole community, where you think, "Yeah, that can happen here." And it's hard when you're very ashamed of yourself to stand up and say, "Yeah, we screwed up." Instead we start making excuses, and pointing the blame at somebody else or others—we do that as individuals, we do it as a community, we do it as a nation. And that's what I think we've done.

SUSAN SWAPP: But still it would be wrong to think that the whole community believes that it wasn't a hate crime.

NARRATOR: Laramie resident Susan Swapp.

SUSAN SWAPP: That would be an unfair characterization of Laramie. I don't believe that. That's the kind of thing that people say, "Oh, Laramie believes that it was a robbery or drug deal gone bad." That makes me really angry. And it's not true. I don't believe that.

MOMENT: POTLUCK

LEIGH FONDAKOWSKI: We spoke to John Dorst, a folklorist at the University of Wyoming. We asked him if he had seen the editorial in the *Boomerang* on the anniversary of Matthew's death.

GREG PIEROTTI: And then we asked him, "So as a folklorist, can you tell us how this change in the story occurred here in Laramie?"

JOHN DORST: As a folklorist, I can tell you that there's a desire for communities to own and control their history. And when that gets taken away, a "reaction formation" occurs. You start with more formed things, the facts of the case or the court proceedings. And the folkloric process is one of winnowing and reduction, the paring away of detail until frequently the actual events—something you might call a story—dissipate. And that's what folklorists call the genre of rumor. But can I ask you—what kinds of versions have you heard?

GREG PIEROTTI: Well, Leigh and I were invited to a potluck last night where we talked to several people.

JOHN DORST: And what did they say?

GEORGE: I heard it was a drug deal gone bad. I don't think it was a hate crime. Laramie is not that kind of a community. The Eastern media had an idea of who we are but that's not who we are. It could have happened anywhere.

GREG PIEROTTI: Yes. One of the responses we often get to the play when people see it is "This could be my town. Laramie is just like my town."

GEORGE: That's it. That's right.

GREG PIEROTTI: But does that mean that there is no homophobia in Laramie, or does it mean that there is also homophobia in other towns?

GEORGE: Laramie is not a homophobic community. There might be individuals who are, but we are not a homophobic community.

JOHN DORST: In some ways it's more acceptable to say yes we do have drug problems in a place like Laramie. It's something you can fix. Hatreds and especially homophobic hostilities seem less controllable.

BEN: I still haven't decided either way, but to say this was a hate crime is not taking the context of the situation into consideration.

LEIGH FONDAKOWSKI: What do you mean?

BEN: That these guys were not virtuous. They were in an environment where drugs and promiscuity prevail and nothing good is going to come from a situation like that. Matthew Shepard missed the signs. Those two guys must have been giving off signs that they were not to be trusted, but he missed them.

LEIGH FONDAKOWSKI: How do you know this?

BEN: I've heard from friends, people I know, people I've hung out with who have told me that they were tweaking.

LEIGH FONDAKOWSKI: But the cops determined they were not tweaking, not on drugs.

BEN: Well, the guys I'm talking about, I would believe them over the cops. I don't trust authority figures in general, and I don't trust the Laramie Police.

JOHN DORST: That kind of insider knowledge. That's another way that people claim control over their stories. You know we're the insiders, we know what really happened.

JIM: Those three guys were a train wreck just waiting to happen. I also heard there was something sexual there too.

GREG PIEROTTI: How do you know? You say these things like you know they are facts, but there was a trial with a lot of evidence given that negated a lot of what you are saying.

JIM: Oh. Well, I hadn't heard that. I guess maybe a little bit of fact and fiction that mixes together and that's how you get an urban myth. It's an urban myth.

JOHN DORST: People will back away very quickly if they're putting forward a rumor type thing and you question it further. When you do push back, you are violating the "convention of rumor." People inevitably back away. The convention is that you DON'T contend it. That's one of the reasons that it can circulate as sort of this vague, "I don't know where I heard this." It's just sort of in the air. It's just around. That's the nature of rumor. So how do you have a certain degree of sympathy for a community that has been traumatized in this way? And at the same time not abandon the ethical and moral position that you would want to take against these rumors? It's a very messy business.

So for me, this is definitely the issue—maybe the core issue here in Laramie—the desire for control over memory or over history.

SUSAN SWAPP: But still it would be wrong to think that the whole community believes that it wasn't a hate crime.

NARRATOR: Laramie resident Susan Swapp.

SUSAN SWAPP: That would be an unfair characterization of Laramie. I don't believe that. That's the kind of thing that people say, "Oh, Laramie believes that it was a robbery or drug deal gone bad." And it's not true. I don't believe that.

BETH LOFFREDA: Of course this story is getting retold.

NARRATOR: Beth Loffreda.

BETH LOFFREDA: Not just here, but nationally. I mean, a Congresswoman from North Carolina just claimed that calling Matthew Shepard's murder a hate crime was a "hoax." So I find it enraging, this idea that it's okay to enmesh us in these dishonesties. Where does that stop? It inflicts real damage to the world we live in, when we all agree to lie, so that we don't have to feel sympathy for someone that so many people feel it's more proper to be disgusted by. I just think it's awful.

MOMENT: NIKKI ELDER

NIKKI ELDER: When Matthew was killed, my oldest daughter was a preschooler.

NARRATOR: Nikki Elder, Laramie High School teacher.

NIKKI ELDER: Now she's fifteen and she has this wonderful friend, this sweet boy, and recently they were on the bus, and these other boys say to him, "Oh, we should just tie you to a fence on the outskirts of town." These other boys said that to this boy. They're high school kids now so they were what, four or five years old when Matt was killed? My daughter reported them, and I am very proud of her for that, and the principal pulled them right in. This is something that was taken very seriously in Laramie. But ten years later, you see the cycle happening again.

MOMENT: THE INVESTIGATING OFFICERS
(Acting note: DEBREE and O'MALLEY should not be played as defensive here. They are confident in the facts and should display all the authority of their offices.)

ANDY PARIS: After hearing so many rumors about what happened that night we decided to talk to the officers who investigated Matthew's case: Rob DeBree and Dave O'Malley.
    We are hearing other people say that McKinney and Henderson didn't target Matthew Shepard because he was gay.

DAVE O'MALLEY: Their own statement was, they went into a bathroom, they hatched the plan to pretend that they were gay, to try to befriend Matt, get him isolated. Okay.

ROB DEBREE: Henderson went into great detail as to how they planned it. . . . They knew he was gay, that one of them would pretend to be gay in hopes of luring him out. You're definitely focusing on an individual because you assume he is gay.

ANDY PARIS: But we keep hearing this was a robbery gone bad. That Henderson and McKinney only wanted money.

ROB DEBREE: That's the beginning, and granted robbery was a part of it, but it went way beyond that. Matthew would have given his wallet to McKinney a few blocks from the bar. That's right up here on the corner, and that would have been the end of the robbery. It went way beyond the wallet.

DAVE O'MALLEY: McKinney's own statement is, "I only had to hit him one time to get his wallet." But then *why* drive this young man out of the city limits, tie him to a fence and hit him in the head and face nineteen to twenty-one times with the butt end of a great big gun.

ANDY PARIS: How else would you answer these rumors?

ROB DEBREE: A lot of people never got to see the crime scene except for law enforcement. The attack point—it was a true battle. They tie him, they beat him viciously. In fact his watch is located almost thirty feet away from him. You could see the marks of blood spatterings in a wide variety of different areas. About twenty yards. We found blood spatter all over. And

Henderson made the statement that Matthew broke free and tried to run. But of course didn't get very far.

ANDY PARIS: But several people have said that McKinney and Henderson were involved with drugs that night.

ROB DEBREE: We've proven that there was no drugs on board with McKinney and Henderson . . . just NONE. Even through their own statements the last time they did the meth was two to three weeks prior. We had blood samples from both of them that night because they both ended up in the hospital. *(Frustrated)* That was a proved thing at the trial. . . . Look, I wish people had seen. When McKinney was in a detention facility he had no problem telling everybody he had killed the faggot . . . he was his own little hero. In fact, the day of his sentencing he was smiling. He had just said, supposedly, that he felt so bad for the family, for what he had done, but he goes over in the detention facility and he's smiling to the other prisoners. So . . . I don't care what McKinney tries to come up with now, or Henderson. I really don't care. I have been in law enforcement going on my twenty-seventh year. . . . I don't know how many times I've addressed it. I don't know what we need to do to get people to understand.

CATHERINE CONNOLLY: We in Laramie need to understand our history and our place in history.

NARRATOR: Catherine Connolly.

CATHERINE CONNOLLY: It's important for us to do that, and we will do that. We MUST do that.

NARRATOR: Stephen Belber.

STEPHEN BELBER: After meeting with Russell's grandmother, I took her advice and wrote to him asking if I could visit and interview him. I heard nothing for three weeks. But today I received the following letter:

RUSSELL HENDERSON: Dear Mr. Belber, I got your letter and I've considered your proposal to talk with me and I've decided that I will do it.

As you know, I've been reluctant to talk to anyone. But I think if there is something I might say that will help someone else to understand or to maybe help them not make the same mistakes I did, then it will be worth it.

I must admit that I'm not the best with words so I don't know how much I will be able to help but I will tell you that I will be honest with you.

I haven't read or seen the play but maybe once you finish this new part of it you could send me a copy of it.

Respectfully, Russell.

END OF ACT I

ACT II

MOMENT: RUSSELL HENDERSON

(Acting note: Be careful not to take on a brooding quality when playing RUSSELL. *The scene should play briskly.)*

NARRATOR: Russell Henderson was the first of the two perpetrators to go to trial in Laramie. He was convicted of murder and kidnapping and is serving two consecutive life terms in prison.

STEPHEN BELBER: The folks at the prison's visitor entrance pat me down, lock up my valuables, and stamp my hand. And then I'm ushered though an outdoor corridor, into a vestibule, where doors shut behind me, before another pair opens before me. And then I enter into the visitors' room where I see Russell, sitting at the table with the low partition. He has no attitude, no show. Just a balding, thirty-year-old man in a green jumpsuit.

RUSSELL HENDERSON: Me and Aaron worked together at the roofing company for about three months before that night. We hung out a fair amount. I was working at the Conoco and the roofing place at the same time.

STEPHEN BELBER: Had you ever gotten into drugs?

RUSSELL HENDERSON: Not really. I've never been on like a drug binge.

STEPHEN BELBER: One of the things people keep saying about that night, with Matthew, is that you guys were on the back end of a two-week meth binge.

RUSSELL HENDERSON: *I* wasn't. The last time I'd done any drugs was on my birthday, which was two weeks before that night. And I'd only done a little bit. I don't know about Aaron.

STEPHEN BELBER: And had you ever robbed people before?

RUSSELL HENDERSON: Never. I mean, I was one of those guys who was brought up with values, but I actually *believed* them. I *believed* the values, I was raised not to hurt people, and I agreed.

STEPHEN BELBER: So why'd you go along with Aaron that night?

RUSSELL HENDERSON: At first I told Aaron I didn't want to. I kept saying no. But he kept wanting to, so finally I just, I went along.

STEPHEN BELBER: Why?

RUSSELL HENDERSON: I guess I'm more of a follower. And he's a leader. So I just went along.

STEPHEN BELBER: Okay, but when you did rob Matthew, why did you take him to the fence? I mean, you had his wallet in the truck, no?

RUSSELL HENDERSON: We were just gonna rob him and leave him out there, so that he'd be stuck out there.

STEPHEN BELBER: Can you tell me what happened when you got out to the fence?

RUSSELL HENDERSON: Aaron told me to tie him to the fence. But I didn't actually tie him. I just wrapped the rope around his hands. Because, you know, I figured . . . I wanted him to be able to leave.

STEPHEN BELBER: And so, when Aaron started hitting him over and over—?

RUSSELL HENDERSON: I just wanted it to stop. I wanted to hide. Make it go away. So I just did what I always did. I hid. Tried to escape. Pretend like it's not happening. Instead of being more . . . strong. I didn't think I could stop him. That's why I went back to the truck.

STEPHEN BELBER: Well one story I've always heard is that you tried to stop him from beating Matthew.

RUSSELL HENDERSON: *(A nod)* Let's just say I tried to stop him but I didn't try enough. You know what I mean? I didn't. . . . It's mostly just, you know, shame. That I didn't do more.

STEPHEN BELBER: What do you wish you'd have done differently?

RUSSELL HENDERSON: I wish I'd have stopped him. I made the wrong choice to go along with it from the beginning; I made the wrong choice to tie him up, I made the wrong choice not to get help. I've thought a lot about it, about every single thing I did; and I just wish I could . . . change what I did.

STEPHEN BELBER: Your grandmother told me you'd taken a victim empathy course?

RUSSELL HENDERSON: Yeah. And what they have you do is actually draft a letter to your victim. Which I did, and I chose Matthew's family, because even though Matthew was my victim, so was his family. And a part of that is that you write about a time in your life when *you* were a victim.

STEPHEN BELBER: What did you write about for when *you* were a victim?

RUSSELL HENDERSON: About when my mom was killed. Which was, obviously, different circumstances, and a different level of attention, but, you know, we both lost family members, in violent crimes. . . .

STEPHEN BELBER: Can you tell me more about how your mom died?

RUSSELL HENDERSON: My mom was killed in Laramie; she was raped, and then the guy just left her on the side of the road. She tried to make it back to town, but she froze to death. . . . Writing about that really . . . helped me, it made me understand the pain I had caused to Matt and to Matt's parents and family.

STEPHEN BELBER: Is that the letter you tried to send to Judy Shepard?

RUSSELL HENDERSON: It . . . prepared me for what I wrote her.

STEPHEN BELBER: And did you ever hear back from her?

RUSSELL HENDERSON: I don't even know if she read it.

STEPHEN BELBER: What do you say to people who say you're just saying you're sorry now because you want your sentence reduced?

RUSSELL HENDERSON: I don't know. I can't really do anything about that. For a long time all I thought about and what I was sorry for was the whole world hating me. But now, all I would want to say to you is that I'm sorry for what I did to Matt's family. That's what I would want to say.

I still have trouble about what I did, what I didn't do, and how I'm going to deal with that for the rest of my life. I still wake up; I'm still trying to figure it out, why I did what I did.

STEPHEN BELBER: As you think about your future, do you, you know, do you have hope?

RUSSELL HENDERSON: *Hope?*

STEPHEN BELBER: Yeah.

RUSSELL HENDERSON: For what?

STEPHEN BELBER: I dunno. To get out?

RUSSELL HENDERSON: No. I don't have hope for that. Mostly no. I try to just accept it.

STEPHEN BELBER: Are you at all religious?

RUSSELL HENDERSON: I mean, I grew up as a Mormon, and my grandmother still is. She's really involved with the church, but after this all happened, I got excommunicated. And so I've had trouble sort of dealing with that.

STEPHEN BELBER: So what went wrong, Russell?

RUSSELL HENDERSON: The only explanation I can offer is I was young and I thought I was strong and I could handle whatever the world could throw at me, and when this happened I realized that none of this was true. I was weak and scared and all I did was hide from it. Every day I play out in my mind what I could have done or what I should have done but none of it matters because I didn't do it.

STEPHEN BELBER: How's your relationship with Aaron these days?

RUSSELL HENDERSON: We're cordial. You know, we're sort of attached forever by this thing, so. . . . He has his friends, I have mine, but we see each other every day. We're cordial. . . . I mean, he's a character, you know? He's the one people are gonna want to hear.

MOMENT: INSTITUTIONAL CHANGE

CATHERINE CONNOLLY: There was certainly the hope and the desire that something like this would never happen again but then you just constantly see the stats of hate crime violence; violence towards gays in this country is going up, not down.

And we still haven't passed any kind of hate crimes legislation in this state.

But one shouldn't be naïve—we certainly know from any kind of social movement that we still have racism, we still have sexism, those haven't gone away.

There's a whole lot more that needs to be done and I'm a person who believes in institutional change so that's why I'm running for a House seat in the Wyoming legislature.

STEPHEN BELBER: On November fourth, two thousand and eight, Catherine Connolly won that House seat, becoming the first openly gay member of the Wyoming Legislature.

MOMENT: LANGUAGE OF DELAY

STEPHEN BELBER: Six months later, we traveled back to Laramie to conduct more interviews. The recession finally caught up with Wyoming. The week we were there, the university announced it had to cut eighteen million dollars from its budget at the request of the governor. The front page of the *Boomerang* announced forty-five people lost their jobs at the university.

Days later, funding for domestic partner benefits finally came to a vote.

From a University of Wyoming press release:

NARRATOR: The University of Wyoming has been considering a domestic partnership initiative for several years now. Today, at a special closed-door meeting the Board of Trustees approved funding for domestic partnership benefits.

(Sotto voce) The approved plan will create a program under which vouchers for health insurance coverage will be offered for domestic partners of either sex of UW employees and is patterned after those at other universities.

ZACKIE SALMON: Woo hoo! Even in the middle of the Wyoming prairie change has occurred!

NARRATOR: Zackie Salmon.

ZACKIE SALMON: It only took ten years! BUT IT PASSED!

BETH LOFFREDA: It's good news.

NARRATOR: Beth Loffreda.

BETH LOFFREDA: The vote was six to five so we feel lucky it came out okay. *But . . .* there is this language of delay in the plan:

NARRATOR: The board's vote directs that the system be implemented only when UW President Tom Buchanan determines it is fiscally feasible to do so. UW recently announced sweeping budget cuts.

BETH LOFFREDA: That language of delay just makes me crazy. As if nobody's getting hurt or burdened while we just wait a little longer. The spectacular dishonesty of people in power who enjoy all of the benefits, right, that they are denying to other people.

MOMENT: DEFENSE OF MARRIAGE ACT (DOMA)

NARRATOR: Leigh Fondakowski.

LEIGH FONDAKOWSKI: We met up again with Cathy Connolly a few months after her term as a representative began to ask her how it was going.

CATHERINE CONNOLLY: Well, I went through freshman training in the House of Representatives, so I'm a freshman. And one of my first orders of business was a Defense of Marriage bill introduced in the House—a Constitutional Amendment; it was one of *those*. Like Proposition Eight in California. Our bill was called Resolution Seventeen, a bill defining marriage in Wyoming as being exclusively between a man and woman.

Bills first must be heard and passed out of a committee before they are debated on the House floor. I testified in that committee against the bill. I came out in that committee. I brought in my son's birth certificate. My son's birth certificate has two women on it, recognized by the State of New York. And I said, *(she holds her son's birth certificate)* "Look, we're recognized as a family unit, and we came here and raised our son and Wyoming didn't fall apart because of it."

But the resolution had enough support to make it out of committee, and therefore it made it to the floor of the House.

CLERK: House Joint Bill Resolution Seventeen: A joint resolution proposing to amend the Wyoming Constitution specifying that a marriage between a man and a woman shall be the only legal union that shall be valid or recognized in the state of Wyoming.

CATHERINE CONNOLLY: The bill was introduced by a Republican, Owen Peterson, so he spoke first:

PETERSON: Mr. Chairman. There are many reasons why the institution of marriage between a man and a woman benefits society. More than thirty years of studies have shown that kids raised by two married biological parents are more successful and better behaved in school, more likely to attend and graduate college, less likely to live in poverty, less likely to drink or do drugs, less likely to commit crimes, less likely to be physically abusive.

Now I can't stand here and say that because there is a marriage between a man and a woman everything is hunky dory with society, that's not the case. But this research has shown that children that have daily access to the daily complimentary ways that mothers and fathers present, studies have shown that that has a definite significant impact, and since I have three children, seven grandchildren, that is definitely the way.

CATHERINE CONNOLLY: And he went on for probably ten minutes . . . and in the Wyoming Legislature, we have a desk mate—and my desk mate, she finally leans over to me and says:

DESK MATE: You don't have to hear this. You don't have to.

CATHERINE CONNOLLY: And I just got up and walked out, but one of my colleagues who is incredibly conservative, I walked by him and he said to me:

CONSERVATIVE COLLEAGUE: *(Note: This was said very gently.)* I'm sorry. This will be over soon.

CATHERINE CONNOLLY: So I went back to my seat.

PETERSON: Mr. Chairman, since the beginning of civilization, in every known society, governments have recognized a marriage between a man and a woman because it provides the next generation outstanding citizens and is the only means of melding two sexes into a stronger and more complete whole.

I exert the body to move forward and pass this resolution. I will relinquish the floor and stand for questions.

CATHERINE CONNOLLY: So that happened. We needed twenty-one votes to strike it down. We had only nineteen Democrats and three or four of them didn't want to do it given their districts. So, we're gonna lose. We're gonna lose. Then another conservative, Representative Childers spoke.

CHILDERS: Ladies and gentlemen, I too have been married forty-six years. I have three lovely children and I'm very proud of them. Two are sons with two granddaughters and another one on the way. My third daughter lives in Montana. *(Pause)* She's gay. She has a significant other. They aren't married because Montana's law doesn't allow it. But folks to my dying breath there's not anybody in this country could say that she is a terrible person, or a something person that needs to be—have their rights restricted. She lives a quiet life with her significant other. Most people would never know she's gay, and quite frankly until she graduated from college my wife and I didn't know it. Her freshman year, very first semester, we had a counselor say she better come home. And why? Well, we had no idea. But she came home because the counselor was very concerned about what was happening to her. And quite frankly I think there was a possibility of suicide. She has grown from that point to a very stable person, and productive and does things for society quite well. She represents a health care faction for the physical therapy association—travels all over the nation. Smart? Oh Lord, she's smart. Good person. But what we're doing with this constitutional amendment, should she have lived here, is to deny her civil rights. You know folks, I grew up in the South. The town that I grew up in was segregated. . . . Now you think about a gay person in redneck country, I can say that 'cause in northeast Texas that's redneck country. And the prejudice against the gay and lesbian community is there I'll guarantee ya. And that hate in their eyes or the fear in the gay person's eyes is there. Do we want a society in this state to do that? Do we want to deny the rights of a gay and lesbian person? I don't think so. Ladies and gentlemen this bill is wrong. And I suggest you vote against it.

CATHERINE CONNOLLY: It was incredibly moving. But at this point we have counts of where we think this was going. So it was gonna pass. We had probably ten or fifteen undecided. And then one last Republican stood up. A very powerful man in Wyoming politics, maybe running for governor in the next election, he got up and he said:

REPUBLICAN MAN: We are the state of Matthew Shepard and the state of *Brokeback Mountain*, but we're also the State of Esther Hobart Morris, first female Justice of the Peace in the United States, and Nellie Tayloe Ross, first woman to serve as a governor of any U.S. state—and—if we let Resolution Seventeen out of this body—our state will be ripped apart at the seams quite frankly. It will divide families, divide churches, divide neighbors, divide friends, and will cause a political havoc that this state hasn't seen in decades. I urge you to vote against this bill.

REPRESENTATIVE COHEE: We have heard this issue and I think it is time to cast the vote. Mr. Chairman, I call for the question.

CATHERINE CONNOLLY: And then came the vote.

CLERK: The question having been called, the chief clerk will call the roll. Peterson.

PETERSON: Aye.

CLERK: Barbuto.

BARBUTO: No.

CLERK: Brechtel.

BRECHTEL: Aye.

CLERK: Brown.

BROWN: No.

CLERK: Blake.

BLAKE: No.

CLERK: Buchanan.

BUCHANAN: Aye.

CLERK: Cannady.

CANNADY: Aye.

CLERK: Childers.

CHILDERS: No.

CLERK: Connolly.

CONNOLLY: No.

CLERK: Davidson.

DAVIDSON: Aye.
(CLERK *goes sotto voce.)*

CLERK: Edmonds.

EDMONDS: Aye.

CLERK: Hallinan.

HALLINAN: Aye.

CLERK: Harshman.

HARSHMAN: Aye.

CLERK: Harvey.

HARVEY: Aye.

CLERK: Hales.

HALES: No.

CLERK: Hammons.

HAMMONS: No.

CLERK: Lockhart.

LOCKHART: Aye.

CLERK: Madden.

MADDEN: Aye.

CLERK: Peasley.

PEASLEY: Aye.

CLERK: Semlek.

SEMLEK: Aye.

CATHERINE CONNOLLY: So we are the state of Matthew Shepard and the state of *Brokeback Mountain* and as ten years has gone on, people resent it—people resent that they are from the place where "that gay kid was killed."
(CLERK comes back to full volume.)

CLERK: Seward.

SEWARD: No.

CLERK: Simpson.

SIMPSON: Aye.

CLERK: Stubson.

STUBSON: Aye.

CLERK: Wallis.

WALLIS: No.

CLERK: That concludes the vote. We will review the count.

CATHERINE CONNOLLY: But in the end—Resolution Seventeen, our Defense of Marriage Bill, didn't pass—it failed by thirty-five to twenty-five. It failed. And it was Republicans. It was Republicans that defeated it.

MOMENT: MEASURING CHANGE #2

NARRATOR: Andy Paris.

ANDY PARIS: We had a chance to talk again with Dave O'Malley, chief investigating officer for the Matthew Shepard case for the Laramie Police Department.

DAVE O'MALLEY: You wanna talk about change? You know, quite frankly before all of this happened, that's how I believed, pretty homophobic. The word "faggot" rolled off my tongue more often than "I love you" to my kids. But after what happened to Matt I was thrust into a situation where I had to interact with the gay community. And those kids were fleeing town. And that was where I started realizing what a hate crime was. I mean look, people get killed in liquor store robberies all the time; but I don't think twice about going in and buying a six-pack of beer. But here kids—and adults too—were leaving Laramie, and that fear, that's when I started realizing—I mean that's . . . that's terroristic. I don't know why it takes a young man like Matt dying for someone like me to start losing my ignorance, but that's what it took.

So, DeBree and I went to Washington seven or eight times with Judy Shepard to advocate for the federal hate crimes bill. But here it is, three administrations later, and the legislation's still not a reality. In nineteen ninety-eight it was called the *Hate Crimes Prevention Act.* In two thousand and seven, it was renamed the *Matthew Shepard and James Byrd, Jr. Hate Crimes Prevention Act.* And when it reached the floor of the House just this year, you won't believe some of the things we heard.

(On upstage screen, video appears of Congresswoman Virginia Foxx.)

VIRGINIA FOXX: *(Video)* The hate crimes bill, that's called the Matthew Shepard bill. It is named after a very unfortunate incident that happened where a young man was killed. But we know that the young man was killed in the commitment of a robbery. It wasn't because he was gay. This bill was named for him. The Hate Crimes bill was named for him. But it—it's really a hoax.

DAVE O'MALLEY: And Judy Shepard was in the gallery that day. And she had to sit there and listen to that.

MOMENT: REMORSE

NARRATOR: Greg Pierotti.

GREG PIEROTTI: Aaron McKinney is in state penitentiary in Virginia. I sent Aaron a letter asking if he would meet with me. I never heard back so I called Father Roger again to see if he could help.

FATHER ROGER: Well, I will send him a letter too. And, Greg, ask Aaron about his remorse. Those of us who have done things in our lives that are really significant in their gravity, we are going to alter our remorse throughout the course of our lives. Sometimes that remorsefulness gets chinked one way, and then it gets bent a different way and then hopefully, by the time we die, we have it in the correct perspective. I think Aaron is not finished finalizing his experience of remorse. And remorse is something we *all* need to think about. So you ask him about that. And, Greg, do him justice.

GREG PIEROTTI: Father, how do I do Aaron McKinney justice?

FATHER ROGER: (*Surprised*) You get to know him, Greg. Let him teach you what it's like to be Aaron McKinney, okay? Now, I will write him today for you.

MOMENT: AARON MCKINNEY

(Acting note: Please do not play AARON *as a sinister or brooding character.* AARON *is a "regular guy" and the tension between what he says and his matter-of-fact disposition is chilling.)*

NARRATOR: Aaron never replied to Father Roger's letter. But Greg put in a request to visit with Aaron anyway, and the prison approved it. Greg went ahead and booked a flight. He went through all the paperwork and questions and metal detectors and pat downs. As Greg headed into the prison, he still didn't know if Aaron was going to see him. But as he passed through the last sally port to the visiting room, there Aaron was, in the very first seat. He had very bright green eyes and a lot of tattoos on his arms. One on his right forearm said: "Trust No One."

AARON MCKINNEY: That's it. You can't reach over the partition again.

GREG PIEROTTI: Oh, okay. Thank you so much for seeing me, Aaron.

AARON MCKINNEY: I threw your letter out, I thought you were the media. And there was no way I was gonna talk to you. I hate the fuckin' media. But when I got the letter from Father Roger that you were friends of him I thought—okay yeah. I'll see you. Father Roger is a good guy, he is definitely family.

GREG PIEROTTI: Yeah, I love Father Roger.

AARON MCKINNEY: Yeah. A big smile and the wind blowing back his face, that's my picture of Father Roger.

GREG PIEROTTI: Those are amazing tattoos you have.

AARON MCKINNEY: Thanks. Yeah. A couple'a guys in here do real good work. Homemade ink, hook a guitar string up to a battery. But it's not allowed, so you gotta have someone watching for the guards and you always gotta stop when they come so it takes forever. I'm working on a full shirt.

GREG PIEROTTI: Wow. That's cool. So, uh, you know we wrote a play and that you are a character in it, right?

AARON MCKINNEY: Yeah, I heard about it. I heard about it, but I never saw it. I don't know what I say in it.

GREG PIEROTTI: Well, it's all your words. We used your actual words from when Rob DeBree interviewed you. That was all we had of yours. What was in the trial transcripts.

AARON MCKINNEY: *(Apparently genuinely surprised)* The trial transcripts?

GREG PIEROTTI: Because when we were interviewing people we couldn't actually speak to you.

AARON MCKINNEY: Okay.

GREG PIEROTTI: And we are checking back with the characters ten years later. So that's why I am here.

AARON MCKINNEY: Okay.

GREG PIEROTTI: So what's it been like in prison for you all this time?

AARON MCKINNEY: This place isn't too good. It's freezing. *(Pointing to his thin green jumpsuit)* This and a real thin blanket is all you get even for outside and in the winter. It's fucking freezing. And they keep us in our cells here all but one hour a day.

GREG PIEROTTI: What do you do for twenty-three hours a day in your cell?

AARON MCKINNEY: Nothin' much. Work out, sleep, watch TV. I don't read much. I read a couple of books. I read *Ice Man,* did you ever read that?

GREG PIEROTTI: No.

AARON MCKINNEY: It's great, man. It's about this hit man for the mob. And then I read a couple of books about the Nazis. They were pretty informative. I'm pretty interested in that.

GREG PIEROTTI: Okay. And what about the other places you have been?

AARON MCKINNEY: Well, they've moved me and Russ like five times. We are always together.
    Wyoming was shit. Nevada was kind of scary. A lot of gangs. Got moved to Texas twice. Texas was a dream, man. It was pretty free. I wish I could get put back in Texas.

GREG PIEROTTI: Is there any chance that you will?

AARON MCKINNEY: No telling.

GREG PIEROTTI: And is there any chance as far as your lawyers are concerned that you will get out of prison altogether?

AARON MCKINNEY: Man, I'm never getting outta here. You kiddin'? I am like the poster child for hate crime murders. Shit, for years, after anything happened to a gay person they thrown my picture up there too. I'm never gettin' out. And you gotta resign yourself to it or you go crazy. So you just try to enjoy yourself. Russ might get out. Shit, he should get out. He doesn't belong in here.

GREG PIEROTTI: Do you see much of him in here?

AARON MCKINNEY: Every day. He is a good friend. I'd give my life for Russ. He didn't do anything. I told him, I would do anything in my power to get him out of here.

GREG PIEROTTI: So he didn't do anything that night?

AARON MCKINNEY: Nothing.

GREG PIEROTTI: Can you talk more about what did happen that night?

AARON MCKINNEY: Well, I have a pretty bad memory of the whole thing.

GREG PIEROTTI: So what do you remember, Aaron?

AARON MCKINNEY: We definitely picked him up to rob him. I was dealing at the time, and I had just got this beautiful gun. Almost brand new Smith and Wesson three fifty-seven Magnum with a ten-inch barrel. Fucking huge beautiful gun. So we went to the Fireside and I was definitely in the mind-set to rob.

GREG PIEROTTI: So you were looking for someone to rob?

AARON MCKINNEY: Yeah.

GREG PIEROTTI: So why Matt?

AARON MCKINNEY: Well, he was overly friendly. And he was obviously gay. That played a part in the part of his weakness. His frailty. And he was dressed nice. Looked like he had money. I think he was drinkin' Heineken. Some expensive beer. And it looked like he had a buncha money in his wallet. It only ended up being about thirty dollars. But so, when he asked us for a ride, I said definitely, man. It was gonna be easy.

GREG PIEROTTI: Okay. So it started as a robbery. But you said you picked Matt because he was gay and you've said many times that you don't like gay people.

AARON MCKINNEY: I don't.

GREG PIEROTTI: So it sounds like his being gay did have something to do with it.

AARON MCKINNEY: It's a possibility. The night I did it, I did have hatred for homosexuals. That mighta played a small part.

GREG PIEROTTI: So you're telling me hatred toward gays played a part.

AARON MCKINNEY: It might have played a small part, yeah.

GREG PIEROTTI: In your initial interview with Rob DeBree, you said he slid his hand like he was going to grab your balls and that was why you started hitting him.

AARON MCKINNEY: I said that?

GREG PIEROTTI: In your interview.

AARON MCKINNEY: Then it might have happened. I barely remember that interview at all. That's what I said?

GREG PIEROTTI: That's definitely what you said.

AARON MCKINNEY: Maybe that happened. Like I said, I barely remember anything.

GREG PIEROTTI: What do you remember? You got him in the truck . . .

AARON MCKINNEY: Yeah, so we got him in the truck and we're drivin'. I had the gun back behind the seat. And I reached back, grabbed it, stuck it in his face, you know, like "rob time." I even poked him in the eye with it. You want to be aggressive when you're robbin' folks, so they believe you'll follow through.

GREG PIEROTTI: *(Somewhat speechless)* So . . . you made him give you his wallet.

AARON MCKINNEY: Yeah, I made him give me his wallet. I do remember one thing that was eerie. He didn't seem scared at all. He was just looking at me. Even when I was hitting him in the truck, *(he bangs his fist into the center of his forehead)* he just kept staring at me.

GREG PIEROTTI: But you were doing some pretty scary things, Aaron. You stuck a huge three fifty-seven Magnum in his face. You poked him in the eye with it, hit him in the head with it. Couldn't he have just been in shock?

AARON MCKINNEY: I never thought'a that. Yeah maybe. He was complying with my demands. But even when I tied him up to the fence, it was odd too. He really didn't seem to be scared.

GREG PIEROTTI: So what happened next?

AARON MCKINNEY: I took the gun by the barrel, so I was holding it like a bat. And I just beat him in the head with it.

GREG PIEROTTI: Okay.

AARON MCKINNEY: Yeah. Then he made a real weird noise and slumped over—you know like they say people make a noise when they give up the ghost.

GREG PIEROTTI: But he didn't give up the ghost. He held on for six more days.

AARON MCKINNEY: Yeah.

GREG PIEROTTI: Okay. So I just want to go back a minute. You said you tied him up?

AARON MCKINNEY: Yeah, to the fence.

GREG PIEROTTI: Okay, in Russ's statement he said that he tied Matt to the fence.

AARON MCKINNEY: Yeah?

GREG PIEROTTI: Yeah.

AARON MCKINNEY: *(Pause)* Well, I don't know. If Russell says he did something then he did it. Russ is a man of his word. But I know I tied him.

GREG PIEROTTI: And so what about the hate crime issue?

AARON MCKINNEY: I don't like gay people, it's true. But as long as they stay outta my way, I got no problem with them. I mean there's guys in here that do that. Nobody really jumps you 'cause you're gay. Unless you're a sex predator. They're like the lowest rung. They get problems here from everyone.

GREG PIEROTTI: Okay. So, let me ask you, in Russell's statement when he pled guilty he told the court he was sorry and felt he deserved to pay the price for what he did. But in your trial you never made much of a statement and so I'm wondering—

AARON MCKINNEY: Do I have remorse?

GREG PIEROTTI: Yes, yeah.

AARON MCKINNEY: You mean do I have remorse? Yeah I got remorse. My dad taught me I should stand tall and be a man. I got remorse that I didn't live the way my dad taught me to live. That I wasn't the man my dad wanted me to be. As far as Matt is concerned, I don't have any remorse. I heard that Matt was a sex predator, and that he preyed on younger guys and had sex with 'em. So when I heard that I was relieved. People might say I am just trying to justify myself, maybe so. As far as I'm concerned, doin' what he was doin', Matt Shepard needed killin'.

GREG PIEROTTI: *(Pause)* Okay. You know those rumors about Matthew Shepard are not true, Aaron.

AARON MCKINNEY: That's not what I heard.

GREG PIEROTTI: *(Pause)* Okay. So, you have no remorse at all.

AARON MCKINNEY: Actually, I do feel bad for Matt's dad. That must be hard to lose your son.

GREG PIEROTTI: And what about his mom?

AARON MCKINNEY: For her too, yeah. I feel bad. Still she never shuts up about it, and it's been like ten years, man.

GREG PIEROTTI: Well, Aaron, you brutally murdered her son.

AARON MCKINNEY: *(Conceding)* Yeah, I know.

GREG PIEROTTI: *(Pause)* And what about yourself. You have no regret. There is nothing you would change in any way?

AARON MCKINNEY: Hell yeah. All sorts of ways. I was a fucker as a kid. A real fucker. Lied to my dad a lot. I hate that. *(Getting glassy eyed)* I fuckin' hate that. He is the greatest dad ever. All the trouble, the drugs. If I could change it I would. I'd go to high school. Graduate.

GREG PIEROTTI: And what if Father Roger were here with us. Could you look him in the eye and honestly tell him you don't feel remorse for Matt?

AARON MCKINNEY: I'd have to. I would never wanna have to do that. You know how I feel about Father Roger. But I couldn't look him in the eye and not . . . I'd have to tell the truth. I do have remorse, but like I said, for all the wrong reasons. For my dad. For ending up in here. For getting Russ stuck in here. *(Beat)* If I could go back and not be the one who killed him I would. . . . But I am better off in here, myself. I met guys in here with a real sense of honor. Out there, people'll stab you in the back for a nickel bag. Besides, I am a criminal. I should be around criminals. I always was drawn that way. Shit, I remember crawling through people's doggie doors when I was eight years old to steal their shit. I don't know why, but I was always like this. Nature trumps nurture.

GREG PIEROTTI: Did you see your son ever, since the murder?

AARON MCKINNEY: Never seen him since I was locked up.

GREG PIEROTTI: *(Pause)* Um okay. Well, I think we're running out of time, Aaron. Before I leave you, I know you say you're never gonna get out of here. But if you did get out, if you were going to get out, where would you go?

AARON MCKINNEY: Shit, I don't know. Italy, maybe or Germany. I am really interested in Germany. But I got some tattoos, some swastikas, and I got "NAZI" across my lower back, in big Old English lettering—looks amazing. I heard they'll put you in jail for that now in Germany. Italy's beautiful though—I would definitely like to see Italy and New York too. I like skyscrapers and you all got the most. That's where you're from right? You guys are lucky. I wish I could go to New York and look at the skyline from the water.

GREG PIEROTTI: Yeah, I really love New York. It's pretty great there.

AARON MCKINNEY: So you getting any pussy while you're down here in Virginia?

GREG PIEROTTI: Aaron, you should know I'm gay. I thought you realized that.

AARON MCKINNEY: Yeah, I thought maybe you were when I first saw you, but I didn't want to say anything 'cause I didn't want to offend you.

GREG PIEROTTI: That doesn't offend me.

AARON MCKINNEY: Okay. Cool.

GREG PIEROTTI: Well, Aaron, thank you so much for seeing me.

AARON MCKINNEY: Sure, man, like I said, any friend of Father Roger's. Take it easy.

GREG PIEROTTI: You too. Take it easy.

MOMENT: JUDY SHEPARD

MOISÉS KAUFMAN: Ten years ago during the trials of the two perpetrators, we met Dennis and Judy Shepard in Laramie. We saw them day after day in the courtroom as they watched the proceedings, and then faced the endless press conferences and media coverage. I sat down with Judy on July eleventh two thousand and nine for our very first formal interview.
(*To Judy*) Judy, when I met you at the trials you were a very private person. You didn't want to talk publicly. But now you're a very public figure. You've been lecturing around the

country and advocating legislative changes and you've met with Clinton and Obama. How did that happen?

JUDY SHEPARD: I'm just doing . . . what a mother does when you hurt her children.

After Matt was killed, and we started speaking in public, all I could see in people's eyes was fear, and especially among the young people, that they understood that what happened to Matt could just as easily happen to them, no matter where they lived.

People were saying to me: Do something. You have to do something. I don't think I've done anything spectacular. I've told a story, I've kept Matt's story alive.

MOISÉS KAUFMAN: *(Pause)* What can you tell me about him?

JUDY SHEPARD: Well, I think I was pretty sure Matt was gay when he was eight years old. Sometimes, you know, something in the back of your mind. When he dressed up as Dolly Parton for Halloween—for the *third* time. He really worked at it too; he got better each time he did it. He always was very serious about acting. He played the little brother in *Our Town*. When he turned eighteen, he called me in the middle of the night and he said, "Mom, I've got something I've got to tell you." My first reaction was, "What took you so long to tell me?" And he said, "How did you know?" I said, "It's a mom thing."

MOISÉS KAUFMAN: Judy, you know we met with McKinney this time?

JUDY SHEPARD: Yes, I know. It will be interesting to hear what he has to say now. *(Pause)* When Dennis and I made the recommendation to the judge to take the death penalty off the table for Aaron McKinney . . . we did that because we just didn't think taking away another son was going to fix anything. And we didn't think Matt would want that either. But it wasn't entirely altruistic. We also understood that if we took the death penalty off the table, we would never have to deal with McKinney again. No appeals, no nothing—he's just gone. And we didn't want Matt's brother Logan to have to deal with that in his life. He would just be gone. So, when McKinney showed up on *20/20* I thought, this is exactly what we didn't want. Here he is again, saying whatever he wants whether it's the truth or not. Changing his story.

MOISÉS KAUFMAN: The changing of the story seems to have really taken hold in Laramie.

JUDY SHEPARD: Yes. I hear the—hate in people's voice—"they robbed him. How could you say it was a hate crime?" I hear people quote the *20/20* story to me still! So . . . I'm not surprised. I've learned so much about people—what they choose to believe if it makes them feel better. How they have to interpret things to make their own being better, to fit their own image of themselves.

It's not just in Laramie, Moisés, it's nationally too.

MOISÉS KAUFMAN: Yes.

JUDY SHEPARD: Dennis and I were in the gallery when the hate crimes legislation bill was being debated in the U.S. House of Representatives. When Virginia Foxx called Matt's death "a hoax." But honestly, I was expecting it. It was the same rhetoric that we always heard from the opposition, that it wasn't a hate crime; it was the same "changing the story" resurfacing, yet again.

MOISÉS KAUFMAN: Judy, I so vividly remember being at the trial and seeing you then. And now I see this woman and they don't seem like the same person.

JUDY SHEPARD: Yeah. I'm angrier now than I was then. Because it's still happening. *(Begins to cry softly, but does not give in to the tears)* Sorry.

So here I am at the ten-year mark still fighting. I had to adapt so I could keep doing this. Or, the feeling would be that it would have all happened in vain! I wasn't going to let that happen. Plus, doing the work was my survival! It was how I coped with losing Matt. I could keep him with me all the time. And I was talking to someone and they said, "Well don't you think maybe it's time to let go, don't you think you're keeping Matt alive by doing that?" And I said, "Of course I'm keeping him alive by doing this! That's the point!" That is exactly the point. And I can keep telling the same wonderful stories and my friends don't say, "Judy, you told me that story yesterday and the day before that and the day before that." I can just keep telling it.

NARRATOR: On October twenty-eighth, two thousand and nine, just a few months after that interview, Judy stood next to President Barack Obama as he signed the *Matthew Shepard and James Byrd, Jr. Hate Crimes Prevention Act* into law.

MOMENT: LEGACY

ANDY PARIS: We heard that when the owner took down the fence where Matthew Shepard was found, the pieces were incorporated into other fences. So no one knows where the pieces of the original fence are. This is Jonas Slonaker.

JONAS SLONAKER: I remembered where the place was and I would still go back, and it's . . . yeah. The fence is gone. Ten years later and the fence is gone. . . . And ten years of snow and rain have washed through there. I mean it's just a place, in the end I guess. And I decided not to go anymore. I had to let it go.

ANDY PARIS: Dave O'Malley.

DAVE O'MALLEY *(holding a photograph)*: This is a photograph of the fence that my son took, and some people had been out and kind of made a little memorial there and . . . I don't know how many people came to town when I was still working at the police department to visit the fence. But I remember one older man—spent thirty years in the military—had to be in the closet through the whole thing. And Matt's death had a huge impact on him. He was from Vermont and one day he just showed up, and I took him out to the fence. I did that with several people, it was important for them. It was important enough for them to come all the way to Laramie to see it! You know? But other than crime scene photographs, this is the only photograph of the fence that I've got.

NARRATOR: We spend the last day of the trip packing our belongings. We're leaving Laramie for the last time. And I find myself thinking about how this story will be told. And about the people we've met. And I think about Matthew.
    This is Romaine Patterson.
(All the other actors leave the stage. ROMAINE sits in the last chair remaining on the set.)

ROMAINE PATTERSON: At the ten-year anniversary this year they were holding a vigil near my house. And I really wanted to go, but I didn't want to speak. I just wanted to go and be a stranger in the crowd. . . . It's ten years later . . . and I've just . . . it's just really recently that I've started to grieve Matt as a person. There was no time for that in those first years. There wasn't an opportunity to sit down and feel the weight of the loss.

I guess over the years . . . I've kind of defined Matthew in two ways. There's Matt who I knew and the good friend that I had, and then there's Matthew Shepard. And Matthew Shepard is very different from Matt. Matthew Shepard is this iconic hate crime that has happened in our history, and Matthew Shepard is not necessarily about Matt, it's about a community's reaction, it is about the media that followed, it is about the crime, but it's not about Matt. And that was a distinction that I had to make, making my way through this storm over the years, so that I could hold on to who Matt was to me personally, but also to recognize the importance of Matthew Shepard, and that story, and how it was told and will continue to be told throughout the years.

(ROMAINE *gets up and leaves the stage. A light on the empty chair. Black out.*)

END OF PLAY

MOISÉS KAUFMAN is a Tony- and Emmy-nominated director and award-winning playwright. He is also the co-founder and Artistic Director of Tectonic Theater Project.

Mr. Kaufman's plays *Gross Indecency: The Three Trials of Oscar Wilde* and *The Laramie Project* (which he cowrote with the members of Tectonic Theater) have been among the most-performed plays in America over the last decade.

He is also the author of the Tony-nominated play *33 Variations*; *One Arm* (his adaptation of the Tennessee Williams screenplay of the same name); and the short play *London Mosquitoes*.

He has directed numerous plays on Broadway, including *The Heiress* starring Jessica Chastain; *33 Variations* starring Jane Fonda; the Pulitzer Prize–nominated play *Bengal Tiger at the Baghdad Zoo* by Rajiv Joseph, with Robin Williams; and the Pulitzer Prize– and Tony Award–winning *I Am My Own Wife* by Doug Wright, which earned Mr. Kaufman an Obie Award for direction as well as Tony, Outer Critics, Lucille Lortell, and Drama Desk Awards nominations.

Mr. Kaufman also directed the film adaptation of *The Laramie Project*, which aired on HBO and was the opening night selection at the 2002 Sundance Film Festival. The film won a Special Mention at the Berlin Film Festival and he received two Emmy Award nominations for Best Director and Best Writer.

Mr. Kaufman is a Guggenheim Fellow.

LEIGH FONDAKOWSKI (Head Writer, *The Laramie Project*; co-author, *The Laramie Project: Ten Years Later*) has been a member of Tectonic Theater Project since 1995. She is an Emmy nominated coscreenwriter for the adaptation of *The Laramie Project* for HBO, and a co-writer of *The Laramie Project: Ten Years Later.* Other original plays include: *The People's Temple*, based on interviews with the survivors of the 1978 Jonestown tragedy, which premiered under her direction at Berkeley Repertory Theater and received the Will Glickman Award for Best New Play in 2005; *I Think I Like Girls*, which premiered at Encore Theater in San Francisco and was voted one of the top ten plays of 2002 by *The Advocate*; *SPILL,* a play and art installation (cocreated with visual artist Reeva Wortel) based on interviews with the people of southern Louisiana in the wake of the BP oil disaster; and *Casa Cushman,* a new play about the hidden love between women in the nineteenth century, featuring a collection of love letters written by the American actress Charlotte Cushman. Leigh is a 2007 recipient of the NEA/TCG Theatre Residency Program for Playwrights, a 2009 MacDowell Colony Fellow, and a 2010 Imagine Fund Fellow at the University of Minnesota. *Stories from Jonestown,* her first work of creative nonfiction, was published by the University of Minnesota Press in 2013. Leigh is a Teaching Company Member with Tectonic.

STEPHEN BELBER's (Associate Writer, *The Laramie Project*; co-author, *The Laramie Project: Ten Years Later*) plays have been produced on Broadway and in over twenty-five countries. His plays include *The Power of Duff; Match; Tape; Don't Go Gentle; Dusk Rings a Bell; McReele; A Small, Melodramatic Story; Geometry of Fire; Fault Lines; One Million Butterflies; Finally; The Muscles in Our Toes; The Transparency of Val;* and *Carol Mulroney.* Movies include *Tape, The Laramie Project* (Associate Writer), *Drifting*

Elegant, Management, and *Match,* the last two of which he also directed, starring Jennifer Aniston and Patrick Stewart, respectively. Television credits include *Rescue Me, Law & Order: SVU,* and pilots for HBO and F/X.

STEPHEN WANGH (Associate Writer, *The Laramie Project*) is a playwright, director, and teacher of acting. The author of fifteen plays, Steve was one of the writers of *The People's Temple* (Glickman Award: Best Play in the Bay Area, 2005), and was dramaturg of Moisés Kaufman's *Gross Indecency: The Three Trials of Oscar Wilde.* Other plays include *(Re)Production* and *Testimony: Scenes from An American Apocalypse.*

He is the author of two books, *An Acrobat of the Heart: A Physical Approach to Acting Inspired by the Work of Jerzy Grotowski* (Vintage, 2000) and *The Heart of Teaching: Empowering Students in the Performing Arts* (Routledge, 2012), and was a translator of Paul Binnerts' *Acting in Real Time.*

Steve has directed in Boston, New York, Boulder, and in Graz, Austria. He has taught acting at Emerson College, Naropa University, and at the Lasalle College of Art in Singapore. He is Arts Professor Emeritus at the New York University Tisch School of the Arts.

More information at: *https://files.nyu.edu/sw1/public/*

AMANDA GRONICH (Dramaturg, *The Laramie Project*) has been a member of Tectonic Theater Project since 2009. Ms. Gronich also originated those roles attributed to her name, performing them in each of the play's original stagings, including its run Off-Broadway at New York's Union Square Theatre. A native of Manhattan, Ms. Gronich received her acting training BA at New York University. She directed Moisés Kaufman's *Gross Indecency: The Three Trials of Oscar Wilde* at Toronto's Canadian Stage Company. Ms. Gronich has appeared in numerous New York theater productions and was a featured lead in the Nick Nolte film *Weeds,* as well as in the HBO Films version of *The Laramie Project.* She records voiceovers for commercials and animation and is the recipient of a prestigious award in acting from the National Foundation for Advancement in the Arts. A recent San Francisco transplant, Ms. Gronich made her Bay Area theater debut in Leigh Fondakowski's *I Think I Like Girls.* She performs stand-up comedy and is coauthor of the sketch comedy revue *We Took a Tour.* Ms. Gronich is also the creator of an original method of acting that she teaches to students on both coasts.

JOHN MCADAMS (Dramaturg, *The Laramie Project*) is a native of San Diego and holds an MFA from University of California San Diego. His acting credits include: *How I Learned to Drive* at the Actors Theatre of Louisville; *The Laramie Project* at Sundance, The Denver Center for the Arts, The Union Square Theatre, and the University of Wyoming; original cast member of *Gross Indecency: The Three Trials of Oscar Wilde* and *Mud, River, Stone* at Playwrights Horizons; and, on television, *Law and Order.* Off-Off Broadway credits include: *A Devil Inside* and *Wally's Ghost* at SoHo Rep, *Jail Bait* at the Women's InterArt Annex, *Downwinders* with Clubbed Thumb, and *Vortex du Plaisir* at the Ohio Theatre.

ANDY PARIS (Dramaturg, *The Laramie Project*; co-author, *The Laramie Project: Ten Years Later*) has made a career of developing new works for the stage and screen, including *The Laramie Project: Ten Years Later, The Laramie Project* (Emmy Nomination), *Gross Indecency: The Three Trials of Oscar Wilde* by Moisés Kaufman, *Or,* by Liz Duffy Adams; Lucie Tiberghien's *The Quiet Room, Innocents* by Rachel Dickstein, The Talking Band's *The Necklace,* Matthew Maguire's *Phaedre*, and Deb Margolin's *Indelible Flesh*. As a writer/director: *Going Public; The American Family* (Edinburgh Fringe); *The Fanmaker's Inquisition*, co-adapted with his lovely wife Anushka Paris-Carter from the novel by Rikki Ducornet; *Goldstar, Ohio* (Director, Cleveland Public Theatre); *Migration* at the Experimental Theatre Wing at NYU; Faith Pilger's *The Stages of Burning;* and *The Corporate Carnival* (Women's Project). Currently he is co-writing a play about living on the autism spectrum, also with Ms. Paris-Carter. Andy has performed in countless other plays in New York, regionally, and in Europe. He has been seen at Denver Center, The Huntington, Playmaker's Rep, Cincinnati Playhouse, Rep. Theatre of St. Louis, Hartford Stage, Theatre Virginia, Berkeley Rep, and La Jolla Playhouse. Favorite roles include Berowne in *Love's Labours Lost*, Keppler in Richard Goodwin's *Two Men of Florence*, directed by Edward Hall, and all the men in *A Sleeping Country*, by Melanie Marnich, directed by Mark Rucker. Film/TV credits include *The Laramie Project* (HBO) and *Law & Order* (NBC). He has also been the recipient of two Audie Awards for his audiobook narrations. Andy was born and raised in Cincinnati, Ohio, and is a graduate of NYU.

BARBARA PITTS-MCADAMS (Dramaturg, *The Laramie Project*) has been involved with *The Laramie Project* in all phases of its development (Sundance Theater Lab; Denver Center; Off-Broadway at the Union Square Theatre; Laramie, Wyoming; Berkeley Rep; La Jolla Playhouse; and the HBO film). She has been involved in the creation of new plays in New York City since 1994, as an active member in the Circle Rep Lab, and as an associate director for New Georges (1996 Obie Award for new work by women). With New Georges she has appeared in Susan Bernfield's *Nice Chair* and Leigh Fondakowski's *I Think I Like Girls* (also Encore Theater/Black Sheep in San Francisco). Barbara's solo Dorothy Parker show *Excuse My Dust* (cowritten and directed by Linda Ames Key) has performed in New York, Pennsylvania, Maine, Washington, and was a finalist for selection at Actors Theater of Louisville's Flying Solo Festival. Selected regional credits as an actor: *The Cherry Orchard, The Birthday Party, The Sound and the Fury, Macbeth* (Lady Macbeth), *As You Like It, Taming of the Shrew* (Kate), *Antigone, Lysistrata, Travesties.* On television her credits include: *Law & Order* and Comedy Central's *Pulp Comics* (with Wendy Liebman). Barbara has taught acting in many settings and authored numerous short plays for Scholastic's *Storyworks* magazine.

KELLI SIMPKINS (Dramaturg, *The Laramie Project*) is a company member of Tectonic Theater Project and is one of the original creator/performers of *The Laramie Project* (directed by Moisés Kaufman)—Off-Broadway, Denver Center, Berkeley Rep, LaJolla Playhouse. She is also an artistic associate of About Face Theater in Chicago, as well as a member of the Study Group. Theater credits: *Spill* (dramaturg/lead performer) at Swine Palace Theater in Louisiana (directed by Leigh Fondakowski); *Teddy Ferrara* (directed by Evan Cabnet) at Goodman Theatre; *The Kid Thing* (directed by Joanie Schultz) at Chicago Dramatists (Jeff nomination for principal actor); *Pony* (directed by Bonnie Metzgar) at Chopin Theater; *In Darfur* (directed by Nick Bowling) at Timeline Theater; *Late: A Cowboy Song* (directed by Jessica Thebus) at Piven; *The Laramie Tour: The Laramie Project* and *The Laramie Project: Ten Years Later; Celebrity Row* (directed by David Cromer) at ATC; *Fair Use* (directed by Meredith McDonough), *Good Boys and True* (directed by Pam McKinnon), and *One Arm* (directed by Moisés Kaufman), all at Steppenwolf Theatre; *Execution of Justice* (directed by Gary Griffon) at About Face Theatre; *The People's Temple* (directed by Leigh Fondakowski) at The Guthrie, Perseverance and Berkeley Rep, and *I Think I Like Girls* (directed by

Leigh Fondakowski) at HERE Arts Center, Cherry Lane Theater. Directing: *Good Death*, an original play that she directed and co-wrote with students at Western Michigan University. Film/ TV: *Betrayal, A League of Their Own, Chasing Amy, Law & Order: Criminal Intent*, and HBO's *The Laramie Project* (Emmy nomination: Ensemble Writing.) She is a certified teacher in Tectonic's "moment work" technique. Kelli is a proud recipient of the 2013 Chicago 3Arts Award.

MAUDE MITCHELL's (Dramaturg, *The Laramie Project*) previous work with Moisés Kaufman includes Queen Elizabeth in *Marlowe's Eye*. She has enjoyed collaborating with other writer/directors as well, including Leigh Fondakowski, Joe Calarco, Lee Breuer, and Adam Rapp. Ms. Mitchell worked in Korea on a Mabou Mines project and recently was a guest artist at Juilliard in a new Adam Rapp play.

SARAH LAMBERT (Dramaturg, *The Laramie Project*) is a member of Tectonic Theater Project (though usually working as a set designer) and has designed multiple workshops and productions of *Gross Indecency: The Three Trials of Oscar Wilde* (New York, San Francisco, Los Angeles, Toronto, and London) and *Marlowe's Eye* (New York). She also designed *Spectators at an Event*, a dance piece by Susan Marshall & Company, performed in Brooklyn Academy of Music's Next Wave Festival. Based primarily in New York, she is an Artistic Associate with the Theater of Necessity, and also a Resident Designer for the National Asian-American Theatre Company, where she designed *Othello*. Other projects include *Much Ado About Nothing* at Cornell and *The Lucky Chance* at Marymount Manhattan. She has also designed for the Mark Tapor Forum, Seattle Repertory Theatre, Playmaker's Repertory

Company, and the Yale Repertory Theatre, as well as for New York University, Barnard College, Hunter College, City College, and numerous downtown New York City companies. She has a BA from Cornell and an MFA from Yale.

GREG PIEROTTI (Associate Writer, *The Laramie Project*; co-author, *The Laramie Project: Ten Years Later*) has been writing, acting, directing, and teaching in the theater for twenty years. He is an associate writer of *The Laramie Project*, and a co-writer of the teleplay adapted for HBO (Emmy and GLAAD award nominations). He is the head writer of *The People's Temple*, for which he and his collaborators received the Will Glickman Playwrights Award. He is a co-author of *The Laramie Project: Ten Years Later*. He has developed his own work and work with Tectonic at Arena Stage, The Magic, the Atlantic Theatre Company, the Sundance Theatre Lab, New York Theatre Workshop, and NYTW summer writers' lab at Dartmouth. His current project, *Apology*, a play based on the life and works of the New York artist Allan Bridge, has been developed at The Orchard Project; Dora Maar House in Menerbes, France; and at Berkeley Rep's Ground Floor. He is a 2013 nominee for the Alpert Award in the Arts for his contributions to the American theater.

JIMMY MAIZE is a writer, director, and has been a member of Tectonic Theater Project since 2003. With Tectonic he has participated in the long-term development of *33 Variations* (Broadway, Arena Stage, La Jolla Playhouse), *One Arm* (The New Group, Steppenwolf), *The Laramie Project: Ten Years Later* (BAM, Lincoln Center), and he teaches Moment Work internationally. Other directing credits include his critically acclaimed 100-actor adaptation of *Spoon River Anthology* (The Invisible Dog, Columbia Stages), *Much Ado About Nothing* and *The Tempest* (Classic Stage Co), the rock musical *Hypochondria* by Kyle Jarrow, and his adaptations of *A Dream Play* and *The Seagull* (Columbia University). Writing credits include *Burn the End* (The New School), *Between Life and Nowhere* (Old Vic, 3-Legged Dog), *In the Belly* (Player's Loft), *In One Room* (Bailiwick Rep), and *John Muir Wolf* (Whitman College). He holds an MFA in directing from Columbia University's School of the Arts.

TECTONIC THEATER PROJECT is an award-winning company whose plays have been performed around the world. The company is dedicated to developing innovative works that explore theatrical language and form, fostering an artistic dialogue on the social, political, and human issues that affect us all. In service to this goal, Tectonic supports readings, workshops, and full theatrical productions, as well as training for students around the country in our play-making techniques.

Founded in 1991 by Moisés Kaufman and Jeffrey LaHoste, "Tectonic" refers to the art and science of structure and was chosen to emphasize the company's interest in new forms of theater. Since its founding, the company has created a series of plays which have sparked national dialogue and inspired artists and audiences worldwide. They include: *Gross Indecency: The Three Trials of Oscar Wilde*, *The Laramie Project* (also an HBO movie, honored with four Emmy nominations, the National Board of Review Award for Outstanding Made for Television Movie, and a Golden Bear Award from the Berlin Film Festival), *I Am My Own Wife* (2004 Pulitzer Prize and Tony Award for Best Play), Tennessee Williams's unproduced screenplay *One Arm* at Steppenwolf Theater, and *33 Variations*.

Other productions include *The Tallest Tree in the Forest*, a dynamic solo work from Obie-winning writer, singer, and performer Daniel Beaty about the life and legend of Paul Robeson; *Square Peg Round Hole,* company member Andy Paris and Anuska Paris-Carter's immersive and visually arresting play about life on the autism spectrum; and *Carmen,* a collaboration between Moisés Kaufman and Afro-Cuban jazz legend Arturo O'Farrill, a re-imagining of the timeless opera set to an Afro-Cuban jazz score.

Tectonic provides training year-round in Moment Work, a technique for creating and analyzing theater exploring traditional theatrical elements (light, sound, props, text) in a unique way. It pushes writers, actors, designers, and directors to collaborate in the making of work, and is the process used in making *The Laramie Project Cycle* plays. The technique breaks apart the traditional roles of theater artists, enfranchising artists of all disciplines to be part of the whole creative process and to be true investigators of the possibilities of the medium.

ACKNOWLEDGMENTS

The members of Tectonic Theater Project and Moisés Kaufman thank the following people for their contributions to *The Laramie Project:*

Michael Emerson, Sarah Lambert, Maude Mitchell, Molly Powell, James Asher, Dave McKennan, Ledlie Hoffstedler, and Jan Leslie Harding for their participation at different stages of the play's development.

In Laramie, the staff of the Albany County Courthouse, the faculty and staff of the University of Wyoming Theater Department, Catherine Connolly and her family, Rob DeBree, Philip Dubois, Tiffany Edwards, Reggie and Mike Fluty and their family, Ben Fritzen, Matt Galloway, Susanna Goodin, Larry and Carolyne Hazlett, Rebecca Hilliker and Rich Nelson, Stephen Mead Johnson, Phil Labrie, Beth Loffreda, Bob McKee, Bear and Jeri McKinney, Matt Mickelson, Jeffrey Montgomery, Garrett Neergaard, Romaine Patterson, Gene Pratt, Cathy Renna, Zackie Salmon, Jessica Sanchez, Father Roger Schmit, Jedadiah Schultz, Jonas Slonaker, Rulon Stacey, Trish and Ron Steger, Zubaida Ula, Harry Woods, and all the people of Laramie, Wyoming, who so generously opened their hearts and minds to us.

Robert Redford, Philip Himberg, Ken Brecher, Robert Blacker, Beth Nathanson, Shirley Fishman, and the staff of the Sundance Theater Lab. They flew us to their beautiful oasis in the Utah mountains and gave us an artistic environment in which to work. Large sections of this play were written there.

In New York, Jim Nicola and New York Theatre Workshop for their belief in our work and their invitation to participate in their summer retreat at Dartmouth, where even more of this play was written. Dominick Balletta and Performance Associates for their guidance and work on our behalf. Lynne Soffer and Walton Wilson for their excellence.

In Denver, Donovan Marley, Barbara Sellers, Rick Barbour, Chris Wiger, and everyone at the Denver Center Theatre Company for producing the world premiere of *The Laramie Project*. They took on a play that was very much in progress—in fact, it had no third act—and gave us a home to finish it.

For their courageous support of the development of the play, we thank Joan Shigekawa and the Rockefeller Foundation, Rob Marx and the Fan Fox and Leslie R. Samuels Foundation, the New York State Council on the Arts, the Jeanne M. Sullivan and Joseph P. Sullivan Foundation, Anne Milliken, and Leon Levy. Roy Gabay, Gayle Francis, Mara Isaacs, Hank Unger, Mike Rego, Matt Rego, John Hart, and Jeff Sharp, who had the vision and know-how to bring *The Laramie Project* to the New York stage.

Joe and Jeanne Sullivan, for their generous and unwavering support of our creative process.

Peter Cane and Joyce Katay for their continuous support and advice; Alan Schuster for his interest and his beautiful theater; and Kevin McAnarney for getting the word out.

To the following people and institutions for their wonderful attention to the very pragmatic things that made *The Laramie Project* possible: Marta Bell, Mérida Castillejo, Randall Kent Cohn, Gino Dilonio, Jonathan Ferrantelli, Michael Honda, Christy Meyer, Megan Spooner, Anne Stott, Courtney Watson, the Atlantic Theater Company, Access Theater, and the Church of St. Paul and St. Andrew.

The Laramie Project Insights:

WORKSHOPS AND RESOURCES TO SUPPORT YOUR PRODUCTION

For schools, universities, and theaters producing *The Laramie Project* and/or *The Laramie Project: Ten Years Later*, Tectonic Theater Project wants to nurture the essential community dialogue that the plays have inspired since their premieres. For this purpose, the Company has developed a program entitled *The Laramie Project Insights*.

The Laramie Project Insights offers three ways to support and engage productions:

1. Laramieproject.org—An online community with resources for people producing, participating in, or interested in *The Laramie Project Cycle*. This site offers members a place to blog, post media, review resource guides for teachers and students, and research information from previous productions. Please visit and join this growing community!

2. Moment Work Training Labs—The Tectonic Company members who created *The Laramie Project Cycle* are available to train your cast in Moment Work, the technique used to build the original production and all of Tectonic's plays.

   Moment Work encourages participants to actively engage with the elements of the stage—exploring lights, sound, costumes, movement, character, text, and architecture—to discover their full theatrical potential and inherent poetry. The technique enfranchises artists to collaborate in creating compelling and theatrical storytelling that utilizes all elements of the stage, to stretch their creative capacity while building a layered narrative in their work.

3. Community Workshops/Resources—In addition to anti-bullying and equality, *The Laramie Project Cycle* touches on many issues beyond the stage, and Tectonic wants to help you develop the resources and programming that will best speak to the needs of your production, audiences, and community members.

TECTONIC THEATER PROJECT ALSO OFFERS THE FOLLOWING
SERVICES:

- Lectures and discussions delivered by Moisés Kaufman and Tectonic Company members
- *The Laramie Project* film viewing and discussion
- Live or virtual Q & A sessions with Tectonic Company members
- Other events and programs to benefit your school, group, or production!

You can also engage with Tectonic through Facebook, Twitter, YouTube, Vimeo, and Flickr.

Interested in learning more? Contact us at:
education@tectonictheaterproject.org
212-579-6111